Digital Image and Audio Communications

Toward a Global Information Infrastructure

Digital Image and Audio Communications

Toward a Global Information Infrastructure

Stanley N. Baron
Mark I. Krivocheev

 VAN NOSTRAND REINHOLD
I(T)P™ A Division of International Thomson Publishing Inc.

New York • Albany • Bonn • Boston • Detroit • London • Madrid • Melbourne
Mexico City • Paris • San Francisco • Singapore • Tokyo • Toronto

CONTENTS

Preface

The year 1995 heralds the 100th anniversary of successful tests of radio transmission. As the 20th century draws to a close, we are about to embark on a revolutionary implementation of the communications industries that grew from those experiments. It is now apparent that the services provided by the broadcasting, telecommunications, and computer industries are converging. This convergence is caused by the shared use of digital technology by these industries. The result of this convergence may be that tomorrow's communications environment will be a continuum of services, with television, telephony, and data information services being brought to the consumer via a global information infrastructure that uses wire, optical fiber, and over-the-air (wireless) technologies. This future global information infrastructure has the potential to provide flexible access to all forms of data, whether that data be image data, sound data, text data, or other forms of information. The current focus is on determining the strategies and tactics on how best to migrate to that tomorrow. All service providers are entering a new era in which the consumers' expectation of the range of services and level of performance will be raised to new heights through noise-free delivery of digital television, sound, and information services. In an era in which the advantages of mobile communications are being expanded and in which consumers will also expect to enhance their participation in the communications experience through various forms of interactivity, the development of practical digital communications using the radio frequency spectrum is becoming increasingly important.

The International Telecommunications Union (ITU), a special agency of the United Nations, is assigned the responsibility for developing international agreements in most of these areas.

The ITU's Radiocommunications Sector (ITU-R) is specifically charged with the standardization of wireless systems and use of the over-the-air frequency spectrum. The ITU's Telecommunications Sector (ITU-T) is specifically charged with the standardization of wired systems such as those used in telephony. This work essentially documents a portion of the ITU's efforts to prepare the essential standards necessary to support a global information infrastructure and to assist the telecommunications industries in meeting the demands for service in the 21st century.

The need to accommodate mobility in the future global information infrastructure means that one of the major focal points is the over-the-air aspect of communications services. The over-the-air media are also the most heavily constrained media. Technical solutions that work in these media and that overcome the combination of noise and interference characteristics and the problem of the limited bandwidth of the available channels will, in general, work in other media environments. Therefore, the focus of the material presented is on technologies and implementations that work in the broadcasting environment but are interoperable with the world of telephony and computers. The mechanisms for achieving that interoperability are also presented.

Digital Image Audio Communications: Toward a Global Information Infrastructure is intended to serve as an information source for students and experts of the communications, television, and broadcasting industries, and for nonbroadcasting communications services. Its primary purpose is to explain how the selected technology works and how it can be applied to developing an information infrastructure. It is also intended to document the historical heritage of the industry and to contribute to the understanding of the forces behind the convergence of the different media into a single information infrastructure.

The authors provide a brief historical overview, focusing on developments in the fields of advanced television (ATV) technologies and services using ITU documents as the basis of the study. The technologies include image and sound compression (bit-rate reduction), and data broadcasting, digital terrestrial television, and satellite broadcasting applications. The advanced television services include high-definition, multiprogram, and interactive television. The authors have organized the work by assembling a collection of landmark ITU documents and providing a narrative text on their importance. Background information on the technology employed is provided so that the reader can understand the use of the digital technology in these applications. The book is not theoretical, nor does it present exhaustive mathematical proofs of the material; instead it provides a comprehensive understanding and summary of the technologies and structures employed and the standards adopted for digital image and sound services. The perspective is from an international point of view and highlights the chronology of the critical developments in the advancement of digital image and sound services.

Acknowledgments

The ideas presented in the book represent work done in hundreds of laboratories and several consortia around the world and made publicly available in the work of the European Digital Video Broadcasting (DVB) project, the Advanced Television Service program, projects organized by the Japanese Broadcasting Technology Association (BTA), the International Organization for Standardization (ISO) and International Electro-technical Commission (IEC) Moving Pictures Experts Group (MPEG), the committees of the Advanced Television Systems Committee (ATSC), European Broadcasting Union (EBU), the International Telecommunications Union (ITU), and the Society of Motion Picture and Television Engineers (SMPTE), among others. This book is a tribute to their individual and collective efforts and the authors congratulate them for the excellence of their efforts.

The book would not have been possible without the permission and support of the International Telecommunications Union (ITU) in providing access to ITU archives and documents. The authors wish to express their profound appreciation to the following individuals at the ITU for their contributions and support in the preparation of this book: Mr. Pekka Tarjanne, Secretary

General; Mr. Richard Kirby, Director of the ITU-R; the members of the staff of the ITU-R in Geneva, Switzerland, and in particular Mr. Richard Nickelson, Senior Counselor; Mr. Giuliano Rossi, Counselor; and Mrs. Renata Zecha. The authors take full responsibility for the contents of this book and although the support of the ITU is acknowledged, it is understood that the support provided does not constitute an endorsement of the factual and intellectual contents of the book by the ITU.

Much of the text of this book was originally created in draft form to accompany the report of ITU Task Group 11/3 on Digital Terrestrial Television Broadcasting, from documents contributed to ITU. The material was reviewed by many contributors and their efforts are gratefully acknowledged, particularly the contributions of Richard Barton (FACTS, Australia), Louis Libin (NBC, U.S.A.), Brian Roberts (TVNZ, New Zealand), and Craig Todd (Dolby, U.S.A.).

The ITU and the SMPTE organized a tutorial program in 1993 on the subject of Digital Terrestrial Television Broadcasting as part of their educational programs. SMPTE has allowed the authors access to the materials developed for the tutorial program, and the efforts of the SMPTE staff in White Plains, New York are acknowledged, and in particular, the Executive Director, Mrs. Lynette Robinson; the Director of Engineering, Mr. Sherwin Becker; and the Editorial Director, Mr. Jeff Friedman.

Progress in the work of Study Group 11 was achieved due to the substantial efforts provided by the members of the Interim Working Parties, the Joint Working Parties, and the Working Groups, and after 1990, by the members of the Working Parties and Task Groups. The creative work of the chairmen and vice chairmen of these committees should also be noted.

1

Introduction

The convergence of telecommunications, broadcasting, and computers is a reality driven by the shared use of digital technology and the demands of a global information economy and society. The latter half of the 20th century has seen the world economy begin a transition from the **Industrial Age** *into the* **Age of Communications**, *thus beginning the establishment of a communications society.*

THE COMING AGE OF COMMUNICATIONS

The past few hundred years are generally referred to as the *Industrial Age*.[1] The industrial age promulgated a way of organizing society (the industrial society) and the economy to meet the needs of the individual and to provide goods and services. An industrial society is characterized by the replacement of manual tools by power-driven machines. In an industrial society, people (human resources), materials, and energy (physical resources) are brought together (concentrated) to work collectively to produce goods and services. In an industrial society, access to those human and physical resources determines the centers of wealth and power. Optimizing society for the industrial model has been reflected in how we organize the communities we live in and our educational systems, as well as the workplace.

In a communications society, knowledge (and its distribution) is considered among the valuable resources. In a communications-based society, human resources and material resources need not necessarily be physically brought together to work collectively to produce the goods and services. In a communications-based society, people may work together at a distance using advanced communications technology to observe and communicate with each other and with intelligent power-driven machines[2] to collectively monitor and modify a process that is occurring in still another location. The organization of a communications society, therefore, may be more dispersed.

The concept of a communications society also allows for a mobile society, one in which individuals may not only work together from different locations, but the location of each individual may not be constant. This concept leads to a requirement for individual, *portable communications appliances* (PCAs).

BROADCASTING: THE MOST TECHNICALLY CONSTRAINED MEDIUM

The need to accommodate mobility in the communications society leads to a focus on the use of the radio-frequency spectrum, the over-the-air aspect of our communications services. Communication services must accommodate all manner of information including text, sound, images, and moving image sequences. A page of text represents perhaps 300 characters and text, therefore, could be transported at the rate of a page a minute using a channel of 40 bits/s (assuming 8-bit representation of the characters). Sound can be sampled at 48 kbits/s and at 16 bits per sample. A monaural sound channel, therefore, could be transported using a channel of 768 kbits/s. An 8x10-in. still image with a resolution of 300 "dots" per inch can be sampled at 10 bits per pixel and transported in 48 seconds at a rate of 1.5 Mbits/s. A standard color television image sequence requires 270 Mbits/s.[3] The ability to transport moving image sequences (television), therefore, represents the most severe communications challenge.

The most efficient way to provide information to the greatest number of users is through the use of a model based on a single point of transmission to multiple receiver points. The mechanism for single-point transmission to multipoint reception is known as broadcasting. The over-the-air broadcast medium is also the most heavily constrained environment. Broadcast services must operate in limited bandwidth channels under noise and interference conditions not found in wired services. Technical solutions that work in the wireless broadcasting environment will work in other, less constrained media. This book, therefore, addresses the work being done in the international community to develop agreements and recommendations on television broadcast services as the basis for an understanding of how technology can be used to support the *Communications Society*. The intent is to provide both an overview of progress made in the application of the technology and a tutorial on the technology itself.

In its beginning, broadcasting simply meant carrying sound over long distances. In February 1939, the essayist E.B. White wrote:

> I live in a strictly rural community, and people
> here speak of "The Radio" in the large sense, with
> an overmeaning. When they say "The Radio" they
> don't mean a cabinet, an electrical phenomenon, or

a man in a studio, they refer to a pervading and somewhat godlike presence which has come into their lives and homes. It is a mighty attractive idol. After all, the church merely holds the remote promise of salvation: the radio tells you if it's going to rain to-morrow.[4]

With the introduction of television, broadcasters transported both moving images and sound from one point to another and provided a visual experience as well as an aural experience. Today, we recognize that broadcasting is an information and data service. In fact, the key to the future of broadcasting is that the move to the application of digital technology allows us to view all services as data services, including vision data and sound data.

The future of all communications is also moving into the realm of interactive multimedia. This implies a future for broadcasting that is both digital in nature and a natural evolution in service from the past. Successful participation in this new world is dependent on the strategy selected and the cost of implementation, which, in turn, are functions of the timing of the event and the technology to be employed.

The migration within the television industry from a reliance on the application of analog technologies to one that is, in the main, based on the application of digital technologies has been evolving over the past 30 years.

Broadcasting and other communications media have come to recognize the advantages inherent in its application. For all communications media, "digital" means reliable and consistent control of service performance, improved immunity from noise, error-free perfect picture and sound propagation within the range of performance, and the opportunity to provide new services. Virtually all communications media are, therefore, increasingly becoming "digital."[5] Consumers have come to expect performance equivalent to that provided by compact disks (CDs) in recorded audio. Consumer receivers and video cassette recorders (VCRs) are becoming available in digital form in the marketplace. Direct broadcast satellite (DBS) services have been launched using digital compression to increase available program service. Cable and telephone companies, using fiber, are retooling to provide digital services and through the use of compression technology offer up to 1500 television channels.

Professor Mark Krivocheev, the Chairman of ITU Radiocommunications (ITU-R) Study Group 11, has written: "We have now arrived at a new era in television broadcasting with many developments arising from work being done on HDTV and digital television systems." Pointing to the ability of digital technology to allow for individual PCAs to provide a diverse number of services, Professor Krivocheev notes that future television receivers, configured to accommodate PCA requirements, would become two-way devices, using narrowband digital return channels. The move toward the standardization of such systems requires a global approach to solutions. PCAs must work in different parts of the world. It is important to design as much compatibility and interoperability into the system as possible. The system must accommodate both broadcasting and nonbroadcast applications equally well. These considerations introduce new challenges in terms of spectrum management: the determination of power levels, interference, and spectrum sharing criteria.[6] Study Group 11 recognizes the need to look at the development of the different forms of enhanced television services in the context of the totality of new developments. The television service environment of the coming years may include enhanced television, high-definition television (HDTV), and even possibly stereoscopic television provided as digital multichannel services and distributed by wire, satellite, and terrestrial transmitters. The goal for a properly designed information infrastructure is to evaluate all methods of delivering information and entertainment services to the consumer and to design compatibility and interoperability into the system to the largest extent possible.[7]

THE KEY TO THE GLOBAL INFORMATION INFRASTRUCTURE

The migration to a digital service is the key issue. Digital technology brings several factors into play:

1. Diversity, the ability to provide multiple services in a single channel
2. Flexibility, the ability to accommodate different levels of services and dynamically alter the service mixture to meet consumer needs
3. Extensibility, the ability to add future services that were not planned at the time the system was implemented
4. Improved and consistent service quality
5. Lower operating cost through use of compression technology.[8]

Digital transmission consists of transmission of streams of data, including vision data and sound data, on what is popularly referred to as the digital highway. Multiple services can be delivered on that digital highway by dividing the continuous data stream into data packets of known length and providing each packet with a header that describes its contents. In this way, the entire data stream can be allocated to different services on a dynamic basis until the entire capacity of the channel is filled. Packets with headers provide diversity, flexibility, and extensibility by allowing the service or function assigned each packet to be individually described. Multiprogramming services can be multiplexed (combined) into a single channel, with each service uniquely identified using packetized data with headers. A packetized data structure facilitates the transfer of image sequences, sound, and data across media boundaries.

Compression is the next key factor. The availability of data space for services is limited. The schemes required to capture an advanced television image and transmit it within a 6-, 7-, or 8-MHz terrestrial channel or to efficiently utilize the data space available on a satellite transponder or contained within recorded material require compression of the data representing the original source images on the order of 70:1.

Even with this level of compression, the data space needed to support the video image in a television service will absorb 75% of the available channel space, and achieving the required level of compression in moving picture sequences without creating unacceptable artifacts in the images is a challenge to the current technology. Limited channel bandwidth places a finite limit on the amount of information that can be placed in a channel. This constraint applies not just to wireless applications. Data space in any medium is a valuable commodity. Compression is a critical technology for all media. Compression not only allows the service to be fitted into a reasonable space but it also dramatically affects the cost.

Digital technology allows the reproduction of the original captured images and sound with greater fidelity and clarity and, through the benefits of compression, uses less resources such as bandwidth or storage space. The implementation of digital technology is still in its infancy, demonstrating a sharply declining cost–performance curve, and that is good news for the future of digital communications.

These views are supported by the findings of the Commission of the European Communities, which listed the potential advantages of "optimally implemented television systems" as including the following:[9]

- interoperability between services. There is the possibility that a properly conceived implementation of digital television could allow easy interworking between television terminals, multimedia workstations, personal computers and other information terminals, resulting in easy and flexible access to a wide range of information services;
- clear and stable pictures and sound;
- efficient use of the electromagnetic spectrum. This is a potentially very important advantage, since spectrum is a finite valuable natural resource with much competition for its use. Some calculations show that with proper planning a gain of between 30 and 40 times in the efficiency of spectrum use can already be achieved with digital techniques;
- flexibility in the provision of television services. Digital techniques allow the configuration of services to be adapted in a flexible manner, allowing a variety of different customer needs to be met when and as required. Indeed, the high bit-rate transmission system developed for digital television could also distribute the digital data for many other applications, thus providing "Integrated Service Digital Broadcasting" (ISDB) services;
- cost considerations. Experience shows that high volume production and higher levels of integration of integrated circuits leads in time to dramatic reductions in unit costs. In a mature market for digital TV, therefore, the prospect exists of high functionality at relatively low cost—as in the computer industry.

The savings achieved through the application of digital compression technology affect both the level of capital investment and operational costs. It is clear that the cost to implement and use digital technology in the communication industries is being reduced by the use of compression technology, advances in computer power, and lower costs of storage.

However, recent experience shows that new technical developments in broadcasting systems are seldom implemented in practice unless they are sufficiently beneficial that the use of the technology provides a return on investment. The creation of standards for new television services must take into account what new kinds of benefits, for both viewers and service providers, justify the costs of the introduction and implementation of new systems and services. This means that new systems must provide additional possibilities for services and features in the television and other information environments.[10]

ORGANIZATION OF THE BOOK

A digital television system differs from an analog system in that analog systems are specific to the application and maintain a single structure (e.g., 525 lines) throughout the production, distribution, and transmission chain. Digital systems can deal simultaneously with different services and different structures and can be configured from different standard modules, the configuration of the modules determining at any point the services provided. It is modularity that allows digital systems to be both flexible and interoperable. The book, therefore, is structured to explain the nature of these modules, their relationships within the digital system chain, and their application when considering specific services.

Chapter 2 provides a general discussion of **the system model** of the future digital television systems, including a discussion of the basic building blocks and why they are necessary.

Chapter 3 discusses **the information transport**, including the service multiplex. The information and service multiplex is the foundation of the system upon which all other modules rest. The chapter introduces the concepts of protocols, packets (of data), and headers (and descriptors), the service multiplex, an explanation of the MPEG transport mechanism, and mechanisms for providing multiprogramming services.

Chapters 4 and 5 provide an overview of **video and audio source coding and compression**, respectively, including an explanation of why compression is required, the basics of video and audio compression technology, methods for coding the video and audio, and an explanation of MPEG video profiles and levels and the MUSICAM and AC-3 audio systems.

Chapter 6, on **modulation**, introduces the methods used to physically transport the digital data stream from the transmission site to the receivers. The chapter reviews the system considerations and discusses the two general approaches available: single carrier systems and the Coded Orthogonal Frequency Division Modulation (COFDM) approach to multiple carrier systems.

Having established the mechanism for providing television services, Chapter 7 discusses **high-definition television (HDTV)** services, which constitute the most difficult service to fit into the broadcast channel.

Chapter 8 discusses various forms of other **advanced television services** such as wide-screen conventional services, multi-program transmission, and stereoscopic television.

Chapter 9 discusses **interactive television services**.

Chapter 10 introduces the work done in **quality assessment and measurement technology**.

Chapter 11 notes the efforts to provide **harmonization and interoperability** between different forms of media.

Chapter 12 draws conclusions on the possible state of **communications in the 21st century**.

Method of Describing MPEG-2 Syntax

The symbols and abbreviations used to describe the MPEG-2 system are those adopted by the MPEG and are similar to those used in the "C" programming language. The syntax descriptors found in this book appear in a smaller font from the normal text. For instance, the elementary stream descriptor field would appear as `elementary_stream_descriptor` in the text.

The following mnemonics are defined to describe the different data types used in the coded bit stream:

`bslbf`   Bit string, left bit first, where "left" is the order in which the bit strings are written. Bit strings are written as a string of 1's and 0's within single quote marks ('1000 1001'). Blanks within a bit string are for ease of reading and have no significance.

`uimsbf`   Unsigned integer, most significant bit first.

The byte order of multi-byte words is: most significant byte first.

THE ROLE OF THE ITU IN CREATING THE GLOBAL INFORMATION INFRASTRUCTURE

The International Telecommunications Union (ITU), a special agency of the United Nations, is assigned the responsibility of developing international agreements and recommendations on both wired and wireless communications. The ITU recognizes the need to consider the changing state of global communication networks and services and develops recommendations for the promotion and harmonization of the worldwide developments in the field.

The majority of the investigations and studies that formed the basis of this book were conducted within the ITU's International Radio Consultative Committee (CCIR) and the ITU's Radiocommunications Sector (ITU-R). The CCIR was created in 1927 for the purpose of serving the needs of the broadcast community and was incorporated into the ITU in 1947. The ITU underwent a reorganization in 1993, and the CCIR was reborn in March of that year as the ITU-R.

FUTURE TRENDS

What trends might this all indicate for the future? We can clearly see that the broadcasting and other wireless communications, telecommunications, and cable and computer industries are converging through the shared use of digital technology. This convergence will make tomorrow's communication environment highly competitive. Developments in mobile radiocommunications means that no place in the world need be devoid of communications services. Television broadcasting, the oldest delivery form of electronic multimedia to the consumer, is entering a new era in which the consumers' expectation of the range of services and level of performance will be raised to new heights.

The availability of an essentially "free" data port on the digital television receiver of the future may place terrestrial broadcasters in the role of leaders rather than followers in the new digital age, for it may be argued that the cost of access to this new digital information infrastructure will determine the service winners and losers, and broadcasting for many years will provide the lowest cost of access per household.

Taking a lead from E.B. White, this convergence of the various media brought about by the adoption of digital technology offers a great opportunity for improved public information services, leaving the public more in awe of the broadcasters' presence than ever before.

END NOTES

1. It is generally accepted that the industrial age began with the industrial revolution, the change in economic and social organization that began in England in 1760. (S.B. Flexner and L.C. Hauck, eds., *Random House Dictionary*, 2nd ed. unabridged, Random House, New York, 1987, p. 976.)

2. An intelligent power-driven machine is defined here as one which is controlled by a computer supported by appropriate software. The computer subsystem may include a means of human interface and remote communication.

3. Based on ITU-RB 601 standard at the 4:2:2 level, with a luminance sampling rate of 13.5 MHz, two color difference signals sampled at 6.75 MHz each, and each sample being of 10 bits resolution.

4. E.B. White, "Sabbath Morn" (essay), *One Man's Meat*, Harper and Brothers, New York, London, 1942, p. 62.

5. P. Tarjanne, Global Television—A Service to Mankind, Keynote lecture, 18th Montreux International Television Symposium, 10 June 1993.

6. M.I. Krivocheev, "A Global Approach to Studies in Television Broadcasting," *EBU Technical Review*, No. 259 (Spring 1994), 24–25.

7. M.I. Krivocheev, Global Options for Enhanced Television, Address to ITU-RB Workshop on Enhanced Television, Auckland, New Zealand, 3–5 October 1993.

8. S. Baron, Digital Television: A Broadcaster's Perspective, Federation of Australian Commercial Television Stations (FACTS) Engineering Seminar, Sydney, Australia, 20 July 1993.

9. Communication from the Commission to the Council and the European Parliament, "Digital Video Broadcasting: A Framework for Community Policy," COM(93) 557 final, Brussels, 17 November 1993.

10. M.I. Krivocheev, Global Options for Enhanced Television, ITU-RB Workshop on Enhanced Television, Auckland, 3–5 October 1993.

2

The System Model

The harmonization of the information infrastructure will make tomorrow's communications environment a continuum of services with television and other data services being brought to the consumer both via wire and through the air. The current focus is on determining the best strategies and tactics to migrate to that tomorrow. All service providers are entering a new era in which the consumers' expectation of the range of services and level of performance will be raised to new heights through noise-free delivery of digital television and other information services. In an era in which the advantage of mobile communications are being expanded and in which the consumers will also expect to enhance their participation in the communications experience through various forms of interactivity, the development of practical digital communications using the radio-frequency spectrum is becoming increasingly more important. The first step in harmonizing the delivery of services to the consumer using a variety of media is the development of a suitable model.

THE SERVICE MODEL

In addressing the harmonization of digital methods for delivery of services to the home,[1] the International Telecommunications Union (ITU) recognized that the technology involved in digital methods for the delivery of services was undergoing and would continue to undergo rapid development. The ITU also recognized that the various delivery methods over terrestrial broadcast channels, cable, satellite channels, via telephony services, and recorded media have different characteristics and require differing transmission (modulation) solutions. The ITU also addressed the need for services to be available at differing levels of quality appropriate to specific applications. In searching for a coordinated approach to the development of such delivery systems, the ITU recommended[2] that source coding and transport mechanisms should be based on common processing algorithms and have a maximum of shared parameters, that the mechanism employed allow use of receivers having differing levels of capability, and that headers and descriptors be included in the data stream to enable the receiver to identify and process a range of services having differing characteristics.

Figure 2-1 provides a service model for delivery of programming that accommodates the concepts of convergence and harmonization. This model separates the digital communications system into a series of interconnected modules. In this model, services (Program Sources) at various levels of performance are digitally encoded, multiplexed into a digital data stream (Service Multiplex and Transport), and distributed through various transmission media (Distribution Interface) to the consumer.

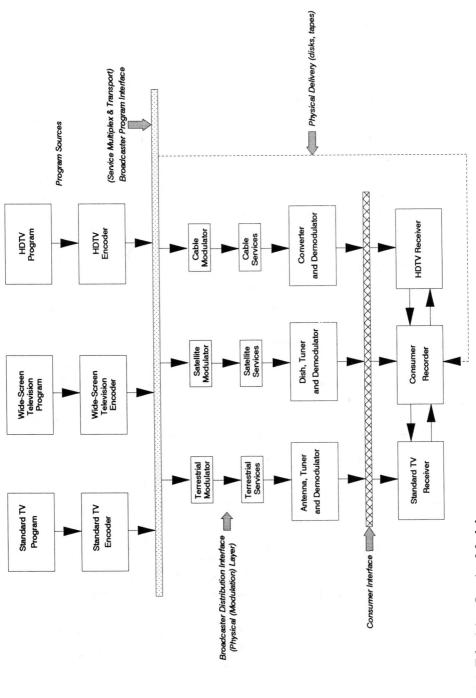

Figure 2-1. Television Service Model.

THE SERVICE PLATFORM

Digital television service developments focus primarily on the quality of the imaging characteristics of the new medium. However, television is a medium that transports both moving images, sound, and data from one point to another, and consideration of appropriate audio and ancillary data services to accompany the television service is a very important part of the implementation process. The implementation of digital television services means development of new standards. Standards for new services emphasizing the transportation of information in a digital format offer opportunities to establish a *new platform for services.*

The primary premise for any platform is that the services provided in each instance should be appropriate to the needs of the individual consumers and should respect the realities of the marketplace. Therefore, the focus should be centered on providing the necessary flexibility to meet those individual marketplace requirements.

In order to meet those needs, these new platforms for services must have certain characteristics:

1. They must have a basic set of standard features and capabilities that are well defined.
2. They must foster innovations that make the services easy to use.
3. They must allow the transport of video, audio, and data across media boundaries.
4. They must be flexible (to allow for local options) and extensible (to provide for future improvements).
5. They must be ubiquitous (present everywhere at the same time).
6. They must be affordable.

COMMUNICATIONS SYSTEMS

A communications system allows the transfer of information from one location to another. In a digital communications system (reference Figure 2-2), the sending or transmission end first converts the analog images and analog sound into digital information as elementary bit streams. The transport subsystem divides the elementary bit streams into packets of data, each packet having a known "length" (number of bits). The transport mechanism also provides suitable individual packet identification in the form of packet "headers" and combines the packetized digital information to form a transport bit stream. The transport bit stream then carries three types of data: image (video) data, sound (audio) data, and associated data such as timing information, program identification, security information, error protection information, captioning information, etc. The digital transport data stream is then sent to the modulator of the transmitter to be converted to a signal that can be transmitted over the air. A receiver recovers the carrier frequency for the specific channel, "demodulates" or extracts the packets of information, separates the packets into separate image, sound, and data elementary streams, and displays the images, recreates the sound, and processes the data, completing the transfer of the information.

Communications systems using digital modulation techniques provide several benefits over systems employing analog techniques. Digital communications systems can provide more immunity from interference and, therefore, can provide a more secure communications link than analog systems. Digital communications systems can be more spectrum efficient than analog systems as they are capable of transmitting more information per channel. In digital communications systems, the information is in a form which facilitates encoding and encryption for applications that require conditional access and security.

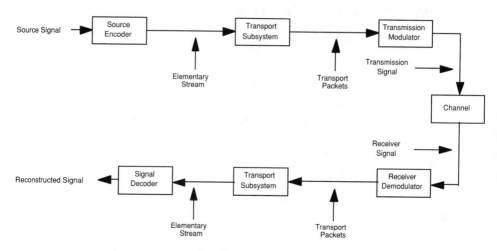

Figure 2-2. Digital Communications System Block Diagram.

THE DIGITAL TERRESTRIAL TELEVISION BROADCASTING (DTTB) MODEL

Within the International Telecommunications Union, Radiocommunications Sector (ITU-R), Task Group 11/3 was charged in January 1992 with responding to the urgent question concerning digital terrestrial television broadcasting.[3] Task Group 11/3, chaired by Mr. Stanley Baron (U.S.A.), met for the first time in Geneva, 14–18 December 1992. The meeting was attended by more than 115 delegates representing 43 Administrations, international organizations, and scientific/industrial organizations. Prior to the meeting, the Task Group Chairman working with four Special Rapporteurs (Mr. Terry Long, United Kingdom; Mr. Osamu Yamada, Japan; Mr. Thomas Ryden, Sweden; and Mr. Richard Barton, Australia) generated an *Outline of Work*[4] as a guide for Administrations and other interested parties preparing documents for consideration at the first meeting of TG11/3 in December 1992 in Geneva.

The outline of work was intended to provide a list of issues which the Task Group should consider in preparing its Recommendations. The document also presented a set of draft Recommendations for consideration, and an outline of a report (or reports) to be generated either as annexes to Recommendations proposed by the Task Group, as Reports to carry the work of the Task Group forward, or in the form of a possible Tutorial Report.

At the suggestion of the chairman of Study Group 11, Task Group 11/3 established a Special Rapporteur, Mr. David Wood (EBU), to globally examine the prospects and methods for achieving a single worldwide digital terrestrial television system. The task involved examining the various elements of the terrestrial television system model, in turn, and reviewing the prospects of obtaining a unique standard in each case. The aim was to decide how likely it was, and how worthwhile it would be, to have single standards and to suggest how this could be achieved in practical terms. The Special Rapporteur produced a document, "Prospects for a common worldwide digital terrestrial television system,"[5] which discusses the process of arriving at a common standard by concentrating on those elements which offer the best combination of priority and ease of agreement.

The outline of work also included a model of a digital terrestrial television broadcasting system. The model was divided into four areas of interest with sub-Task Groups assigned to develop the required Recommendations and Reports. The Task Group used the model as the basis of its investigations.

The four subsystems of the system model are as follows[6] (reference Figure 2-3):

1. Source coding and compression
2. Service multiplex and transport
3. The physical layer (modulation scheme), including the channel coding parameters
4. Planning factors (which include consideration of both the transmission and receiver environments) and implementation strategies.

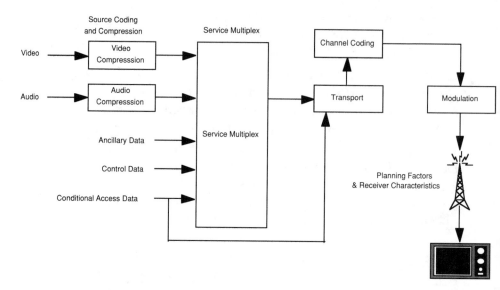

Figure 2-3. The DTTB System Model.

Source coding refers to coding methods designed to reduce the very large data stream created when images are represented by a sequence of values representing the individual picture elements (pels) in the digital domain or when sound is represented by digital audio samples. Source coding may also include error protection techniques that are appropriate for application on the video, audio, and ancillary digital data streams. Source coding involves processes that reduce the bit stream containing the image, sound, or ancillary data information in such a way as to be able to recreate a representation of the original source at the receiving point without noticeable or unacceptable degradation. The term "ancillary data" includes control data, including conditional access control, or data associated with the program audio and video services such as closed captioning. Ancillary data can also refer to independent program services. The purpose of the coder is to convert the audio and video into data and minimize the number of bits needed to represent the information.

The *service multiplex and transport* refers to the means of dividing the digital data stream into "packets" of information, the means of uniquely identifying each packet or packet type, and the appropriate methods of multiplexing the video data stream packets, the audio data stream packets, and the ancillary data stream packets into a single data stream to construct a single program. Multiplexing also provides the capability of combining different program data streams into a single broadcast channel for simultaneous delivery. In developing an appropriate transport mechanism, interoperability between digital media such as terrestrial broadcasting, cable distribution, satellite distribution, recording media, and computer interfaces must be a prime consideration.

The world community has developed a standard, MPEG-2,[7] for the basic coding and multiplexing of video, audio, and data signals for digital broadcasting systems.[8] The MPEG-2 standard was developed for television applications in which channel bandwidth or recording media capacity is limited and the requirement for an efficient transport mechanism is paramount. MPEG-2 is also designed to be compatible with the Asynchronous Transfer Mode (ATM) transport mechanism. ATM was developed for use in the telephony environment, where variable path transmission must be accommodated. The relationship between the two signal formats is discussed in Chapter 11.

The channel coder takes the resulting compressed data bit stream and adds additional information that can be used by the receiver to recognize and reconstruct the images, sound, and ancillary data from the transmitted signal. This module includes mechanisms by which additional data are added to the multiplexed data stream to provide protection against loss of the signal. The characteristics of the channel coder are selected to support the modulation scheme and the medium through which the data must be transported.

The *physical layer* refers to the means of using the digital data stream information to modulate the transmitted signal. Modulation is a mechanism whereby the protected data stream is imposed on one or more carrier signals for transmission. These transmission systems are referred to as single-carrier and multiple-carrier schemes, respectively.

Planning factors and implementation strategies include consideration of the characteristics of the transmission media and receivers and discussions of strategies appropriate for the introduction and implementation of a digital terrestrial television broadcast service, taking into account existing broadcasting services.

MINIMUM STANDARDS SET

To achieve international exchange of program and data services across media boundaries, it is necessary to agree upon a basic set of standards. This set includes the following:

1. A common, multiple-level compression syntax for both video and audio
2. A common program multiplex standard, including the following three standards:

   - A common standard for identification (Headers/Descriptors)
   - A common recording standard for program interchange for each of the levels of compression used
   - A common electrical and mechanical interface standard at the data stream level.

In October 1994, Mr. Baron[9] and Mr. Wood[10] working together developed a Recommendation[11] that provided the basis for agreement on the minimum standards set for a digital terrestrial television broadcasting system. The agreement provided for the following:

- A base system capable of conveying a single HDTV service or a number of conventional quality services.
- Coding video sources in conformance with the MPEG-2 standard at the Main Profile, Main Level (MP/ML) or higher.
- Coding audio sources in conformance either with the MPEG-2 standard Level II or the AC-3 standards, noting that efforts should be made to encourage the development of integrated circuits (ICs) which can decode both types of audio coding. Because these two coding systems were being used by different digital packaged media, a common decoder was seen as a major advantage for the consumer.
- That the service multiplex and transport should conform with the MPEG-2 standard and be based on a common Service information and Header/Descriptor system.
- That the channel coding and modulation scheme should use either the 8-VSB system where single carrier systems are appropriate or COFDM technology where multiple carrier systems are appropriate.

The chapters that follow consider requirements for future telecommunications services and the characteristics of the subsystems (modules) necessary to accommodate the services envisioned.

END NOTES

1. ITU-R [Doc. 11/141], Draft New Recommendation, "Harmonization of Digital Methods for Delivery Systems for Television Services to the Home," Document 11/BL/55-E, 30 March 1994.

2. ITU-R Document 11-3/TEMP/6, Draft New Recommendation, "The Basic Elements of a World-Wide Family of Systems for Digital Terrestrial Television Broadcasting," October 1994.

3. ITU-R, Question 121/11, "Digital Terrestrial Television Broadcasting."

4. CCIR Document 11-3/2, "Outline of Work for Task Group 11/3, Digital Terrestrial Television Broadcasting," 30 June 1992.

5. CCIR Document TG11-3/TEMP/16, "Prospects for a Common Worldwide Digital Terrestrial Television System," 17 December 1992.

6. ITU-R Document TG11/3-2, "Outline of Work for Task Group 11/3, Digital Terrestrial Television Broadcasting," 30 June 1992.

7. IEC/ISO 13818, "Generic Coding of Moving Pictures and Associated Audio Information" (MPEG-2).

8. Chairman, ITU-R Task Group 11/3, "Report of the Second Meeting of ITU-R Task Group 11/3, Geneva, 13–19 October 1993," 5 January 1994, p. 40.

9. ITU-R Document 11-3/TEMP/1, "Chairman's Opening Remarks," October 1994.

10. ITU-R Document 11-3/19, "Recommendation for Main Elements of a Common Digital Terrestrial Television ITU-R Standard," 14 September 1994.

11. ITU-R Document 11/37, Draft New Recommendation, "The Basic Elements of a World-Wide Family of Systems for Digital Terrestrial Television Broadcasting," 2 November 1994.

3

The Information Service Multiplex and Transport[1]

The information service multiplex and transport subsystem provides the foundation for the digital communication system. This subsystem takes the encoded elementary bit streams representing image data, sound data, and ancillary data, forms them into manageable packets of information, provides a mechanism to indicate the start of a packet (synchronization), assigns an appropriate identification code (header) to each packet, and multiplexes the packets into a single transport bit stream.

The transport is constructed in a series of steps. First, the raw digital data is formatted into **elementary bit streams**. Second, the elementary bit streams are formed into **packets** with descriptive headers. The packetized data is then multiplexed into a **program transport stream** which contains all the information for a single program. Multiple program transport streams may then be multiplexed to form a **system level multiplex transport stream**. This chapter describes how the transport subsystem is structured.

AVAILABLE TRANSPORT STRUCTURES

Wireless communications are the most constrained of the communications media; channel bandwidth tends to be limited. For example, the channels assigned to broadcast television services are limited to 6-, 7,- or 8- MHz bandwidth, depending on the region of the world. Further, the channels are both noise and interference limited, requiring careful planning to provide reliable services. In establishing a service multiplex and transport standard for this environment, Task Group 11/3 considered three existing established standards: ATM, integrated services digital broadcasting (ISDB), and MPEG-2.[2]

ATM technology was developed to solve the multiplex and transport problems found in the communications world of telephony. In the ATM structure, information is encapsulated in cells of 53 bytes. The first 5 bytes (the header) contain the multiplexing information and the last 48 bytes (the payload) contain the user information. The ATM standard is designed to function in a switched network, multipath environment. In a multipath environment, different cells of the same message may follow different paths between the source and the receiver. In order to ensure correct end-to-end delivery of the information in the order of transmission, an ATM adaptation layer (AAL) has been defined which supports the message path and node identification and time information necessary to allow proper reconstruction of the messages at the receiving end. However, in the single-path DTTB environment, the bytes allocated to message path identification constitute wasted overhead.

The Japanese Administration proposed application of ISDB to digital broadcasting, noting its inherent flexibility, extensibility, interoperability, good transmission characteristics, easy program reception, conditional access capability, and other features. The ISDB system was originally developed for satellite broadcasting applications, and experimental satellite and terrestrial television and sound systems were developed in Japan using this system.[3]

The Moving Picture Experts Group (MPEG) of ISO/IEC also produced a multiplex structure (MPEG-2), designed initially for use with recorded media and extended for use in DTTB systems. The transport mechanism for the proposed North American[4] and European[5] DTTB systems employ a subset of the MPEG-2 system transport stream syntax.

The MPEG-2 system packet multiplex structures were specifically tailored to the needs of broadcast television services with consideration of compatibility with ATM structures. The MPEG-2 systems packet structure consists of 188 bytes comprised of 4 header bytes and 184 payload bytes. This packet size can be encapsulated within four ATM cells as four 47-byte payloads ($4 \times 47 = 188$), leaving space for one ATM AAL byte per ATM cell. The MPEG-2 system, therefore, transports data with less overhead than the ATM system. Overhead is an important consideration in the highly constrained DTTB environment.

Task Group 11/3 adopted the MPEG-2 structure as the basis of the DTTB service multiplex and transport standard. The discussion in this chapter on multiplex and transport system requirements uses the MPEG-2 system as the model to explain the methodology. The discussion is not intended to be a full exploration of the MPEG-2 system, but uses a subset of the MPEG-2 syntax to explain how a system might be constructed. The reader is directed to document ISO/IEC 13818-1, "Information Technology—Generic Coding of Moving Pictures and Audio, Recommendation H.222.0—Systems," for a full discussion of the subject.

MULTIPLEXING OF VISION, SOUND, AND DATA

Program Stream Versus Transport Stream Multiplexing

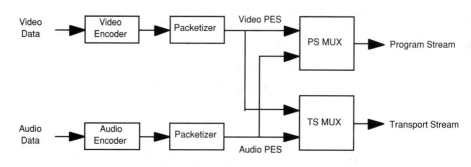

Figure 3-1. Approaches to System Multiplexing.

The signal ensemble in a DTTB system is formed by multiplexing the various component video, audio, and data bit streams that make up the service. As illustrated in Figure 3-1, digitized video and audio data streams, termed **elementary bit streams**, are first formed into variable-length **packet elementary streams** or **PES packets**.

In general, there are two approaches to constructing a single channel representing multiple applications. One approach is based on the use of fixed-length packets and the other on variable-length packetization.

Audio	Video	Audio	Video

Program Stream

Audio	Video	Audio	Video	Video	Video	Audio	Video	Audio	Audio	Video	Video	Video	Audio	Video

Transport Stream

Figure 3-2. Packetization Approaches.

The two multiplexing schemes are motivated by different application requirements. In the program stream approach, packets from various elementary bit streams are multiplexed by transmitting the bits for the complete packets in sequence, resulting in a sequence of variable-length packets in the channel. Program streams were designed for relatively error-free media such as CD-ROMs. MPEG-1 is a program-stream-based system. MPEG-1 was developed giving consideration to the needs of recording media.

In the transport stream approach, PES packets including the PES headers from the various elementary bit streams are carried as a payload within fixed-length transport packets. Each transport packet is accompanied by a transport header that includes bit stream identification information. Each PES packet for a particular elementary bit stream would then occupy a variable number of transport packets, and data from various elementary bit streams are interleaved with each other at the transport packet layer. New PES packets always start a new transport packet, and stuffing bytes (i.e., null bytes) are used to fill packets that are only partially filled with PES data. Transport streams were designed for environments in which errors and data loss events are likely, including certain storage media and transmission on noisy channels.

Figure 3-2 provides examples of bit streams for both the **program stream** and the **transport stream** approaches to demonstrate their differences. The program and transport data streams both address the same general layers of functionality, and, therefore, it is not necessary to carry a program bit stream within a transport bit stream or vice versa. Transcoding between the two formats is feasible, and interfaces between them can be constructed.

Fixed-Length Packetization

The use of fixed-length packets offers a high level of flexibility in allocating channel capacity among video, audio, and data services. The MPEG-2 system makes use of a **packet identification (PID) field** in the packet header as a means of bit stream identification, and this allows a mix of video, audio, and data which need not be specified in advance. The entire channel capacity can be dynamically reallocated to meet immediate service needs, including allocation of the entire bit stream for delivery of a specific service. This **dynamic capacity allocation** functionality is inherent in the DTTB system.

It is important that the transport architecture be open-ended because we cannot anticipate, today, all possible future services. The DTTB system is open-ended. It allows new elementary bit streams to be handled at the transport layer without hardware modifications by assigning new PIDs at the transmitter for new or additional services. Backward compatibility with existing receivers is assured when bit streams with new PIDs are introduced at the source because existing decoders will automatically ignore PIDs that are not part of their instruction set. Newer decoders would respond to the new PIDs as appropriate. This capability could be used to compatibly introduce newer, higher temporal or spatial resolution services or stereoscopic video services by sending augmentation data along with the normal television service data. The presence of multiple elementary bit streams in the data channel with provision for expansion to identify future services allows the system to be **extensible**.

Another fundamental advantage of the fixed-length packetization approach is that the fixed-length packet can form the basis of handling errors that occur during transmission. Error detection and correction processing (which precedes packet demultiplexing in the receiver subsystem) may be synchronized to the packet structure so that data loss due to transmission impairments is handled at the packet level in the decoder. Access to the data stream is restored from the first good packet after an error during transmission. Synchronization information is transmitted in each packet header at fixed and known locations in the bit stream. Recovery of synchronization within each application is also aided by the transport packet header information. Without this approach, recovery of bit stream synchronization would be completely dependent on the properties of each elementary bit stream. The presence of fixed-length packets, therefore, improves the system's **robustness**.

FORMATTING THE INPUT DATA STREAM

Elementary Bit Streams

As stated earlier, video, audio, and other forms of data are presented to the transport as **elementary bit streams**. The format of elementary bit streams is defined for the MPEG-2 system with each elementary stream consisting of a 5-byte fixed-length component and a variable-length `elementary_stream_descriptor` component as shown in Figure 3-3 and described in Table 3-1.

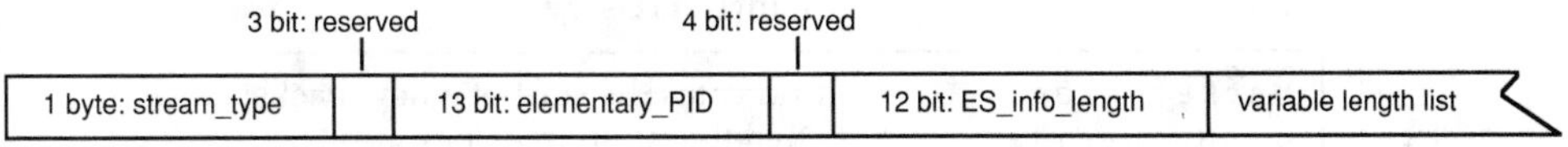

Figure 3-3. Elementary Bit Stream Format.

Table 3-1. Elementary Stream Description.

Field	Function/Usage
`stream_type`	Indicates the application being considered in this elementary stream.
`elementary_PID`	Indicates the PID of the transport bit stream containing the elementary bit stream.
`ES_info_length`	Indicates the length of a variable-length `elementary_stream_descriptor` field that follows.

MPEG-2 PES Packet Format

Prior to entering the transport layer, elementary bit streams may be transformed into PES packets. The PES packet structure is shown in Figure 3-4.

A PES packet begins with a PES_packet_start_code, the unique elementary stream stream_id, and the PES_packet_length. PES packets carrying various types of elementary streams can be multiplexed to form a program or transport stream. The stream_id can take on a number of values indicating the type of data in the payload as shown in Table 3-2.

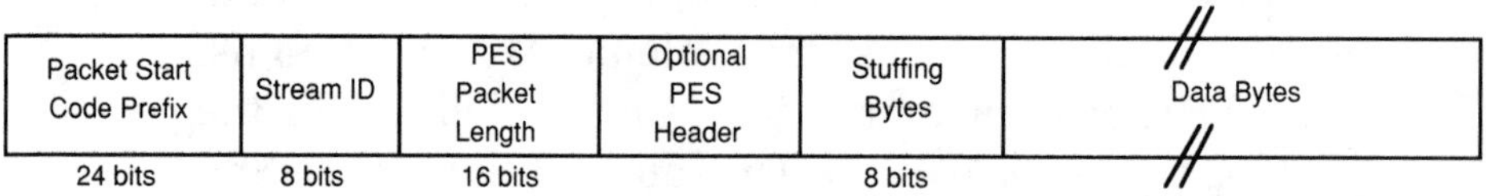

Packet Start Code Prefix	Stream ID	PES Packet Length	Optional PES Header	Stuffing Bytes	Data Bytes
24 bits	8 bits	16 bits		8 bits	

Figure 3-4. PES Packet Format.

Table 3-2. PES Packet Overview.

Field	Function/Usage
packet_start_ code_prefix	Indicates the start of a new packet. Together with the stream_id forms the packet_start_code. Takes the value 0x00 0001.
stream_id	Specifies the type and number of the stream to which the packet belongs: 1011 1100—Reserved stream. 1011 1101—Private stream 1. 1011 1110—Padding stream. 1011 1111—Private stream 2. 110x xxxx—MPEG Audio stream number xxxxx. 1110 xxxx—MPEG Video stream number xxxx. 1111 xxxx—Reserved data stream number xxxx.
PES_packet_length	Specifies the number of bytes remaining in the packet after this field.

The identification information is followed by a description of the PES header contents including PES header flags, PES packet length and header fields, and a data block payload. The PES header flags indicate which fields and what description information is present, and the header fields contain the actual descriptive information. The payload is a stream of contiguous bytes from a single elementary stream. Flags are used in the MPEG system to conserve data space. In general, when a flag is set to "1," the corresponding field is present. When a flag is set to "0," the corresponding field is not present. For instance, if the PES header ESCR flag is "0," the ESCR field is not present, saving 42 bits.

The PES header flags for a constrained example of the MPEG-2 system are shown in Figure 3-5 and described in Table 3-3, and indicate which of the descriptor properties of the bit stream or additional flags are present on the PES header.

Table 3-3. PES Header Flags.

Field	Function/Usage (Each Flag = 1 Bit, Unless Otherwise Noted)
PESSC PES_scrambling_control	2 bits: Indicates the scrambling of the PES packet received. 00: not scrambled; 01–11: user defined.
PESP PES_priority	Indicates priority of this packet with respect to others. 1 = high priority; 0 = no priority.
DAI data_alignment_indicator	Indicates nature of the alignment of the first start code in the payload. The type of data in the payload is indicated by data_stream_align- ment_ descriptor. 1 = aligned; 0 = not aligned.

Table 3-3. (continued)

Field	Function/Usage (Each Flag = 1 Bit, Unless Otherwise Noted)
CY, copyright	Indicates copyright nature of the associated PES packet payload. 1 = copyrighted; 0 = not copyrighted.
OOC original_or_copy	Indicates whether the associated PES packet payload is the original or a copy. 1 = original; 0 = copy.
PTSDTSF PTS_DTS_flags	2 bits: Indicates the presence of PTS or PTS and DTS in the PES header. 00: neither present; 01: PTS field is present; 11: both PTS and DTS are present.
ESCRF ESCR_flag	Indicates presence of Elementary Stream Clock Reference field in the PES header.
ESRFES ES_rate_flag	Indicates whether the Elementary Stream Rate field is present in the PES header.
DSMTMF DSM_trick_mode_flag	Indicates presence of an 8-bit field describing the Digital Storage Media (DSM) operating mode. (For DTTB functions, set = 0.)
ACIF additional_copy_info-flag	Indicates presence of the additional_copy_info field.
PESCRCF PES_CRC_flag	Indicates presence of the CRC field.
PESEXT PES_extension_flag	Set as necessary to indicate that extension flags are set in the PES header. Its uses includes support of private data.

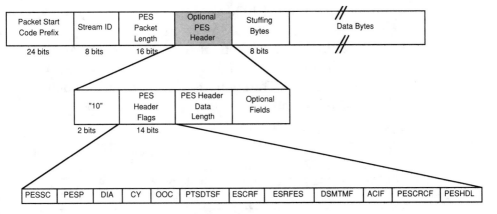

Figure 3-5. PES Header and Flags.

PES header information follows the PES_header_ length field, which indicates the header size in bytes. The size of the header includes all of the header fields including any extension fields and stuffing_bytes. The format is shown in Figure 3-6. The PES header can contain additional flags if the PESEXT flag is set. These flags

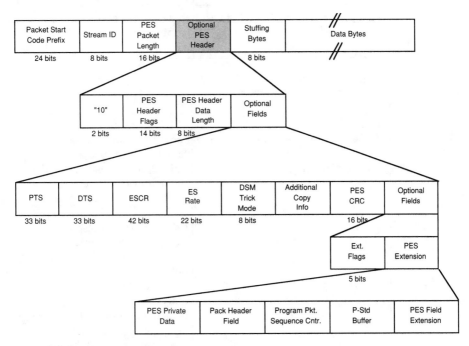

Figure 3-6. PES Extension Fields and Flags.

are transmitted in a 1-byte field as shown in Figure 3-6 and described in Table 3-4. As examples, a DTTB transport of video PES packets usually requires that the `data_alignment_indicator` be set and the `DSM_trick_mode` flag not be set. The contents of the PES header fields are described in Table 3-5.

Table 3-4. PES Extension Flags.

Field	Function/Usage
`PES_private_data_flag`	Indicates whether the PES packet contains private data.
`program_private_ sequence_counter_flag`	Indicates whether an MPEG-1 systems packet header or an MPEG-2 program stream packet header is present.
`STD_buffer_flag`	Indicates whether the `STD_buffer_scale` and the `STD_buffer_size` flags are encoded.
`PES_extension_field_flag`	Indicates the presence of additional data in the PES header.

Table 3-5. PES Header Fields.

Field	Function/Usage
`PTS` (`presentation_time_stamp`) `DTS` (`decoding_time_stamp`)	PTS informs the decoder of the intended time of presentation of the presentation unit. DTS informs the decoder of the intended time of decoding of an access unit. When encoded, PTS refers to the presentation unit corresponding to the first access occurring in the packet. If the access does not occur in the packet, it does not contain a PTS. Under normal conditions, the DTS may be derived from the PTS and need not be encoded. A video access unit occurs if the first

Table 3-5. (continued)

Field	Function/Usage
	byte of the picture start code is present in the PES packet payload. An audio access unit occurs if the first byte of the audio frame is present.
DSM_trick_mode	An 8-bit field indicating the nature of the coded information. The field is further partioned as follows: trick_mode_control (3 bits) field_id (2 bits) intra_slice_refresh (1 bit) frequency_ truncation (2 bits)
trick_mode_control	Indicates the nature of the DSM mode: 000—Fast Forward 001—Slow Motion 011—Fast Reverse 010—Freeze Frame 1xx—Reserved
field_id	This identifier is valid for interlaced pictures only, and indicates how the current frame is to be displayed: 00—Display field 1 only 01—Display field 2 only 10—Display complete frame 11—Reserved
frequency_truncation	This field indicates selection of coefficients from the DSM: 00—Only DC coefficients are sent 01—The first three coefficients in scan order (on average) 10—The first six coefficients in scan order (on average)

Table 3-5. (continued)

Field	Function/Usage
	This field is for information purposes only. At times, more than the specified number of coefficients may be sent. At other times, less than the specified number of coefficients may be sent.
`intra_slice_refresh`	This field indicates that each picture is composed of intraslices with possible gaps between them. The decoder should replace the missing slices by repeating collocated sites from the previously decoded picture.
`field_rep_control`	This field indicates how many times the decoder should repeat field 1 as both the top and bottom fields alternatively. After field 1 is displayed, field 2 is displayed the same number of times. When set to "0," this identifier is equivalent to freeze frame with `field_id` set = 10.

CONSTRUCTING THE PROGRAM TRANSPORT STREAM

In the MPEG-2 system, a **program** is analogous to a broadcast channel programming service. A complete program bit stream can be formed by multiplexing individual transport packetized video, audio, and data elementary bit streams sharing a common time base and a control bit stream (called the **elementary stream map**) that describes the program, as shown in Figure 3-7. Each elementary bit stream and the control bits stream are identified by their unique PIDs in the header field. The elementary stream map contains the `program_map_table` which includes information about the PIDs of the individual streams that make up the program, identifies the applications that are being transmitted on these bit streams, and establishes the relationship between these bit streams. One approach[6] to linking the elementary streams of a program allocates the values of the 13-bit PID field of the transport packet so that associated elementary streams share a base number (nine most significant bits) that identifies the program. The `program_map_table` PID always has bits b_0 through b_3 set to zero (0) and the associated elementary streams are assigned PIDs equal to the base number plus some number ≤ 15 (F_h). The approach is described in Table 3-6 and assumes that programs associated with a single transport multiplex would be numbered 1 through 255.

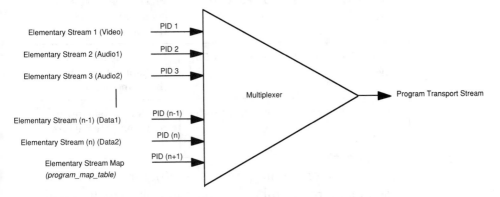

Figure 3-7. Program Transport Stream Multiplex.

The 13-bit PID field is used to indicate the type of data stored in the packet payload. Certain PID values are reserved:

- PID value 0x0000 (PID = 0) is reserved for the Program Association Table (PAT) that maps program identities to the PIDs of the streams containing the `program_map_table` (PMT_PID) for the individual programs, as shown in Table 3-6.
- PID value 0x0001 is reserved for the Conditional Access Table.

- PID values 0x0002– 0x000F are reserved.
- PID value 0xFFFF is reserved for null packets.

Table 3-6. Program PID Assignments.

Name	PID Definition	Description
PMT_PID	base_PID +0x0000h	PID for the bit stream containing the program_map_table for the program
Video_PID	base_PID +0x0001h	PID for the bit stream containing the video for the program
PCR_PID	base_PID +0x0002h	Implies the video bit stream also carries the PCR for the program
Audio(A)_ PID	base_PID +0x0004h	PID for the bit stream containing the audio (A) for the program
Audio(B)_ PID	base_PID +0x0005h	PID for the bit stream containing the audio (B) for the program
Data_PID	base_PID +0x000Ah	PID for the bit stream containing the data for the program

The transport syntax allows a program to be comprised of a large number of elementary bit streams with no restrictions on the types of applications required within a program. A program transport stream does not need to contain compressed video or audio bit streams. It could contain multiple audio bit streams for a given video bit stream. The data applications that can be carried are flexible, the only constraint being that there should be an appropriate stream_id assignment of the application corresponding to the bit stream for recognition by a compatible decoder and that the total data required not exceed the capacity of the channel. This approach to bit stream configuration is compatible with the requirements of storage and playback of programs. Although not directly related to DTTB transmission, the ability to create programs in advance, store them as a compressed multiplexed bit stream, and play them back at the desired time is a desirable feature. The interface between storage and transmission can be very efficiently handled by the use of transport bits streams for both media.

CONSTRUCTING THE PROGRAM SERVICE

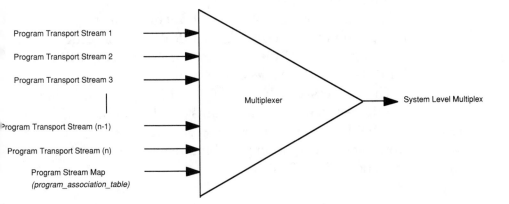

Figure 3-8. Multiple-Program System Multiplex.

The MPEG-2 system also allows multiplexing of different program transport streams to form a multiple-program multiplex. The overall multiplexing scheme can be described as a combination of multiplexing at two different layers. In the first layer, single-program transport streams are formed as previously described. In the second layer, multiple-program transport streams are combined using packet multiplexing to form the overall, multiprogram system. This is made possible through the use of the `program_association_table`. In addition to the transport bit streams with their individual PIDs that define the individual programs, a system level control bit stream with PID = 0 is defined. This bit stream carries the `program_association_table` that maps program identities to their program transport streams. Programs are identified by a number in the program_association_table which points to the PID of the bit stream containing the program_map_table for the program. The process of identifying a specific program and its contents takes place in two stages: first, the program_association_table in the PID = 0 bit stream is used to obtain the program_map_table for the program, and in the next stage, the PIDs of the elementary bit streams that make up the program are extracted from the appropriate program_map_table. This approach to system layering is shown in Figure 3-8.

During the process of system level multiplexing, there is a possibility of receiving identical PIDs on different program streams. This presents a problem because PIDs for different streams need to be unique.

The process can be made scalable by multiplexing multiple-system level bit streams on a higher bandwidth channel by extracting the program_association_tables from each system multiplex bit stream and reconstructing a new PID = 0 bit stream.

FORMING MPEG-2 TRANSPORT PACKETS

Overview

The packetization approach described in this section is based on fixed-length packets that allows a variable length in the header field as shown in Figure 3-9.

In this approach, based on the MPEG-2 standard, each packet consists of 188 bytes (1504 bits). In selecting this size packet, consideration was given to the packet size being large enough so that the overhead due to transport headers did not become a significant portion of the total data carried, and that the packets be limited in size so that the probability of packet error does not become significant under standard operating conditions. A further constraint is that the packet lengths should also be compatible with the size of typical error correction mechanisms. This allows packets to be synchronized to error correction blocks and further allows the physical layers of the system to aid the packet level synchronization process in the decoder. Interoperability with the ATM format was also considered in determining the size of the packet.

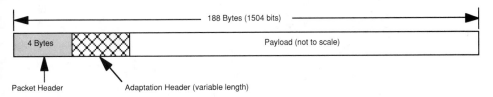

Figure 3-9. MPEG-2 Transport Packet.

The contents of each transport packet and the nature of the data it is carrying are identified by **packet headers**. The packet header structure is described by a fixed-length **link layer** and a variable-length **adaptation layer**. The syntax elements of a possible system transport layer bit stream are defined here for the purpose of exploring the requirements of such a system.

The Link Layer

The link layer is implemented using a 4-byte header field. Figure 3-10 shows a possible link layer header with functionality assigned to each bit. Table 3-7 provides a description of each function. Some of the functions are not necessarily required to support DTTB services but are useful for providing interoperability with other media.

Packet synchronization (the start of a packet) is enabled by the first byte in the packet, the sync_byte. The sync_byte has the same fixed, preassigned value for all DTTB bit streams. The 13-bit packet identifier (**PID**) field that follows provides the mechanism for the multiplexing and demultiplexing of bit streams by enabling identification of packets belonging to a particular elementary or control bit stream. Because the location of the PID field in the header is fixed, extraction of packets corresponding to a particular elementary bit stream can be achieved once packet synchronization is established.

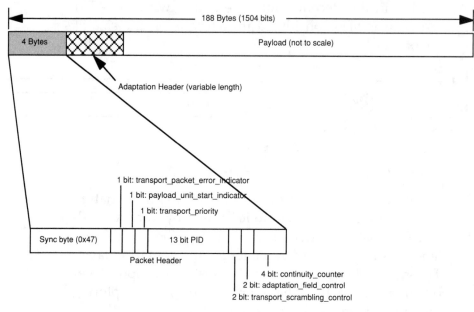

Figure 3-10. Link Header Format.

Error detection can be enabled at the packet layer in the decoder through the use of the `continuity_counter` field. The value of this field is cycled at the transmitter end from 0 to 15 for all packets with the same PID that carry a data payload. At the receiver end, under normal conditions, the reception of packets in a PID stream with a discontinuity in the `continuity_counter` value may indicate that data have been lost in transmission. The transport processor at the decoder then signals the decoder for the particular elementary stream that data may have been lost. The MPEG-2 specification does allow the `continuity_counter` to be discontinuous in order to accommodate downstream insertion of data packets. This downstream capability can be used by local service providers to insert programs or messages of local content into a regional service.

Table 3-7. Link Header Format.

Field	Function/Usage
`sync_byte` (Value: 0 x 47)	Packet synchronization.
`transport_unit_error_indicator`	Indicates if packet is erroneous. 0: no problem, 1: problem packet, payload is not to be used. Can be used for error signaling from modem to transport demultiplexer.
`payload_unit_start_indicator`	Indicates presence of a PES packet header containing program-specific information (PSI) in the payload. The PES packet header always begins the payload of the packet. The starting byte of the PSI table in the packet is indicated using a pointer field; 0: no PES header or start of PES table present, 1: PES header is present.
`transport_priority`	Indicates priority at input to transmission channels which support prioritization. 1: higher priority; 0: lower priority.
`PID`	Packet identifier for multiplex/demultiplex.
`transport_scrambling_control`	2 bits: Indicates the descrambling key to use for the packet. 00: not scrambled; 01: Reserved; 10: "even" key; 11: "odd" key.
`adaptation_field_control`	2 bits: Indicates if an adaptation field follows. 00: Reserved; 01: no adaptation field (payload only); 10: adaptation field only (no payload); 11: adaptation field followed by payload.

Table 3-7. (continued)

Field	Function/Usage
continuity_counter	Increments by one for each packet within a given PID and transport priority. If two consecutive transport packets with the same PID have the same value and the adaptation_ field_control equals 01 or 11, the two transport packets are considered duplicates. Used at the decoder to detect lost packets. Not incremented for packets with adaptation_ field_control of 00 or 10.

The transport format also allows the scrambling of data in the packets, and each elementary bit stream in the system can be scrambled independently. The link header information in the packet is always transmitted in the "clear" (unscrambled). The amount of data to be scrambled in a packet can be made variable depending on the length of the adaptation header. Some padding of the adaptation field might be necessary to accommodate certain block-mode algorithms. One approach to scrambling would be to specify the descrambling method used but not include the descrambling key or how it is to be obtained by the decoder. The descrambling key must then be delivered to the decoder by an alternate means and be available at the time of its intended use. A portion of the "private" data capacity within the DTTB data stream could be used to carry the required additional conditional access data. There is no system-imposed limit on the number of keys that can be used or the rate at which they are changed. The only requirement that might be placed on a receiver is that a standard interface between the decoder and the decryption hardware be defined. Note that the general MPEG-2 transport definition allows scrambling at two levels, within the PES packet structure and at the transport layer.

The Adaptation Layer

An MPEG-2 derived DTTB system adaptation header uses a variable-length field. Its presence is flagged in the link level `adaptation_field_control` field. The adaptation header consists of information useful for higher-level decoding functions and uses flags to indicate the presence of particular extensions to the field. The header begins with a fixed-length component that is present whenever the adaptation header is transmitted, as shown in Figure 3-11.

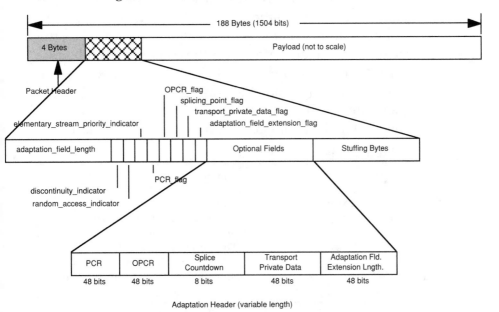

Adaptation Header (variable length)

Figure 3-11. Adaptation Header Field.

The `adaptation_field_length` is a 1-byte field that specifies the number of bytes that follow it in the adaptation header. The `adaptation_field_length` also reflects the number of stuffing bytes. The `adaptation_field_length` can also be used by the decoder to skip over the adaptation header in order to advance to the data payload when appropriate. The presence of additional adaptation header fields is indicated by the state of the last five single-bit flags shown in Figure 3-11. The first three flags do not produce extensions to the adaptation header but provide system status and are described in Table 3-8.

Synchronization of the decoding and presentation process for the applications running in a receiver is an important aspect of real-time digital data delivery systems. The problems in dealing with this issue for a digital compressed bit stream are different than for analog television. In analog television, information is transmitted for the pictures in a synchronous manner, and a "clock" can be derived directly from the picture synchronization information. In a DTTB system, the amount of information generated for each picture is based on the picture coding algorithm and the complexity of the picture and is, therefore, variable in time. Timing cannot be derived directly from the start of the picture data, as there are no display control synchronization pulses in the digital bit stream, as found in analog television.

Table 3-8. Adaptation Header Fields.

Field	Function/Usage
`discontinuity_ indicator`	Indicates there is a discontinuity in the PCR values that will be received from this packet onward. This occurs when bit streams are spliced. This flag should be used at the receiver to change the phase of the local clock.
`random_access_ indicator`	Indicates that the packet contains data that can serve as a random access point into the bit stream. One example is to correspond to the start of sequence header information in the video bit stream.
`elementary_stream_ priority_indicator`	Logical indication of priority of the data transmitted in the packet.

The digital solution is to transmit timing information in the adaptation headers of selected packets to serve as a reference for timing comparison at the decoder. This is done by transmitting a sample of a 27-MHz clock in the `program_clock_reference` (PCR) field, which indicates the expected time at the completion of reading the field from the bit stream at the transport decoder. The phase of the local decoder clock is compared to the PCR value in the bit stream to determine whether the decoding process is synchronized. The audio and video sample clocks in the decoder are locked to the system clock derived from the PCR values, aiding in rapid synchronization at acquisition. The PCR field can be modified during the transmission process. An `original_program_clock` reference (OPCR) provides the same reference information for the recording and playback of a single program and is not modified during the transmission process. The PCR and OPCR fields are described in Figure 3-12. In each case, the 9-bit extension field cycles from 0 to 299 at 27 MHz, at which point the value in the 33-bit field is incremented by 1. This results in the 33-bit field being compatible with the 33-bit field used for the 90-kHz MPEG-1 clock. The cycle time of the PCR and OPCR is approximately 26 hours.

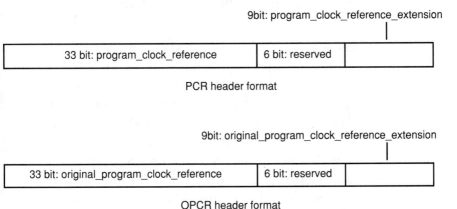

Figure 3-12. PCR and OPCR Header Format.

The `splice_countdown` field is a 1-byte field that is present when the `splicing_point_flag` is set. The `splice_countdown` field indicates the number of packets in the bit stream with the same PID as the current packet until a splicing point packet. The splicing point packet is defined as the packet containing a point in the elementary bit stream from which point data can be removed and replaced by another bit stream. The field contains a twos complement value. The `splice_count-down` field is useful for downstream (local) program insertion.

The `transport_private_data` field is described in Figure 3-13 and is used to carry private, information data packets in the stream.

8 bit: length field (L)	L-byte: transport_private_data or adaptation_field_extension

Figure 3-13. Private Data Header Format.

PROGRAM IDENTIFICATION

The functional layer that contains the program and system level information is called the PSI (program-specific information) layer. A program is received and the contents identified based on the following four tables of the PSI:[7]

1. The `program_map_table` (PMT), which transmits the relationship among the elementary streams that constitute a program, its attributes, and the PID of the packet in which the program is sent.
2. The `network_information_table` (NIT), which transmits the information about the transmission channel in which the program is sent.
3. The `program_association_channel` (PAT), which lists the PIDs where the PMTs and NITs can be found.

4. The `conditional_access_table` (CAT), which provides information on conditional access.

PSI tables are generally transmitted in the appropriate bit stream sequentially, without a gap between the tables. As tables need not necessarily start at the beginning of a transport packet, there needs to be an indicator as to where they begin in the bit stream. This indication is achieved with the `pointer_field`. The `pointer_field` is present in the packet if a PSI table begins in the packet. This event is signaled at the link level by setting the `payload_unit_start_indicator` to 1. The `pointer_field` indicates the number of bytes that follow it before the start of a PSI table. A `pointer_field` value of 0x00 indicates that a new PSI table follows immediately.

The `program_association_table` is transmitted as the payload of the bit stream with PID = 0 and describes how program numbers associated with program services map onto bit streams containing the `program_map_tables` for the indicated programs. The `program_association_table` may be transmitted as multiple `program_association_segments` with each segment having a maximum length of 1024 bytes. The `program_association_table` and `program_association_segments` are described in Figure 3-14 and Table 3-9. The transport decoder can extract individual table segments in whatever order it desires. Each table segment has a fixed 8-byte header component for table segment identification, a variable-length component that depends on the number of entities contained, and a 4-byte CRC-32 field.

The variable-length `program_association_table` list consists of a `program_count` (number of fixed-length entries corresponding to each program) and `stuffing_bytes`. As previously noted, the program identity "0" is reserved for the PID of the bit stream carrying information about the entire system. This bit stream is meant to be a private bit stream. For all other program identities, the `program_map_PID` is the PID of the bit stream containing the `program_map_table` for the particular pro-

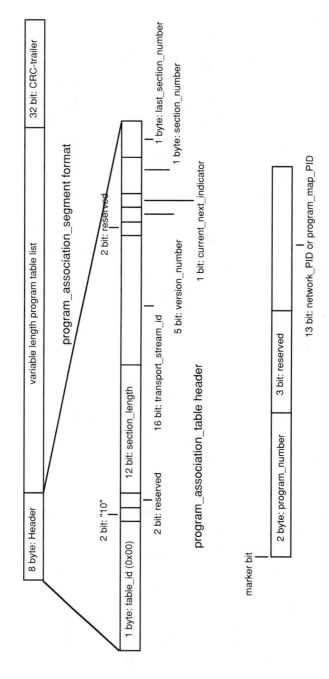

Figure 3-14. Program Association Tables.

gram. The 4-byte CRC field is calculated over the entire map segment starting with the `segment_start_code_prefix`. The CRC is based on the polynomial $X^{32} + X^{26} + X^{23} + X^{22} + X^{16} + X^{12} + X^{11} + X^{10} + X^8 + X^7 + X^5 + X^4 + X^2 + X + 1$.

Table 3-9. Program Association Table Header.

Field	Function/Usage
`table_id`	1 byte: Indicates the nature of the table. 0x00 indicates a `program_association_table`.
`section_length`	12 bits: Length of the `program_association_table`. The length includes all bytes following this field up to and including the CRC. The two most significant bits of the field are set to 00, giving a maximum value of 1024.
`transport_stream_id`	2 bytes: Identifies a particular multiplex from several in the network. Indicates the service number.
`version_number`	5 bits: Incremented each time there is a change in the `program_association_table` being transmitted.
`current_next_indicator`	1 bit: 1 indicates that the map is valid; 0 indicates that the map is not currently in use.
`section_number`	1 byte: Identifies the particular section being transmitted.
`last_section_number`	1 byte: `Section_number` for the last section in the `program_association_table`.

In the transport stream (TS), the `program_map_table` is transmitted as the payload of the bit stream with a PID equal to the `program_map_PID` as indicated in the `program_association_table`. The `program_map_table` carries information about the applications that make up the programs. Each `program_map_table` is transmitted as a single `TS_program_map_section`, as shown in Figure 3-15. The format for a `TS_program_map_section` contains an overall header field, fields that describe each program within the table, and a CRC field. The CRC is the same as that used for the `program_association_table`. Each `program_map_PID` may contain more than one `TS_program_map_section`, with each of the latter describing a different program.

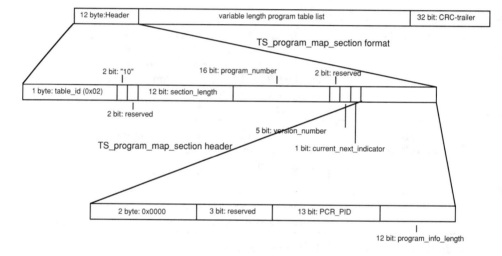

Figure 3-15. TS (Transport Stream) Program Map Format.

The header for the `TS_program_map_section` consists of the `table_id` field (0x02), 2-bytes used to identify the `program_number` of the program being described, a 13-bit `PCR_PID` which identifies the PID of the particular packetized elementary bit stream in the program containing the PCR values, and the `program_info_length` field, which indicates the number of bytes of program descriptors that follow. All other fields have the same format and functionality as found in the `program_association_table`.[8]

Network Information Table (NIT)

The NIT indicates the service, transport ID, channel frequency, and other channel information but is not, as yet, specified in the MPEG-2 standard. In wireless services, two essential functions are assumed by the consumer as being accommodated. They are the function of receiving a channel continuously and the function of simultaneously recording an individual program. Therefore, Task Group 11/3 agreed that it was necessary to define a new descriptor, called the "Event Descriptor," to identify individual programs because the MPEG-2 provided program_number corresponds to the program channel. The Task Group proposal for the descriptor is shown in Figure 3-16.[9]

8-bit: descriptor tag	8-bit: descriptor length	32-bit: event id

Figure 3-16. Network Information Table-Event Descriptor.

FEATURES AND SERVICES

Introduction

The DTTB transport architecture is flexible and can support a number of audio, video, and data services through its system multiplex. In practice, data services may be program related or nonprogram related. The Society of Motion Pictures and Television Engineers and others have identified program-related data services that could be communicated from the program source and would be helpful to display of the program. The identified functions would be used by the receiver to improve the system performance and to enhance the service for the viewer. Some of the functions are viewed as useful in distribution networks to support international program exchange, for scalable service environments, or for use in a simulcast implementation scenario.

Audio Compression Types and Language Identification

The transport layer syntax allows the definition of a program map permitting identification of individual audio services by their compression algorithm as well as identification of multiple-language channels that can be selected by the viewer or by the distribution network. This requirement to identify compression algorithms allows selection of an audio service (monaural, stereo, or surround sound) and bit rate appropriate to the associated program.

Navigational Guides

The ability to carry multiple programs on a single broadcast channel will increase both the number of choices available to the viewer and the complexity of the program selection process. The ITU is addressing the requirements for a uniform navigational guide.[10] The solution must consider an environment where the choice of programming channels may exceed 300 or more. This implies a standard accessing method based on the availability of a stored database within the receiver appliance. Program service information can be provided as an ancillary data service with its own PID. The proposed database could contain information on all programs on all programming channels available from all sources if the content provider so desired. Then programs could be sorted for presentation to the viewer for selection by source, by date and time, by title, by program content, and so forth with a multilevel, menu-oriented selection scheme. The existence of such a capability within the digital receiver implies an appropriate level of intelligence built into the receiver. Such a level of intelligence is very possible considering the computing power that must be resident in the receiver to decode a transport stream and restore the original video, audio, and data services for presentation.

Captioning

Captioning information, like audio services associated with the video, must be synchronized with each television frame. Captioning information may be uniquely identified and carried as user data within the video picture layer or as a separate private data stream.

Closed Captioning

Closed captioning is a captioning service designed for the hearing impaired. Like general captioning information, closed captioning services must be synchronized with each television frame and may be uniquely identified and carried as user data within the video picture layer. However, nothing in the MPEG-2 syntax would prevent closed captioning data from being sent in a separate PID, and in some applications it might have some advantage over carrying the data within the video picture layer.

Program Source and Program Identification

Information concerning program source and program identification has many uses. One application is to allow automatic access to programming for recording and delayed playback by the viewer. ITU-R Working Party 11D investigated the types of program information data that a digital broadcasting service might support:[11]

- Identification of service (programming channel) and programs (or individual program events) and program components (image and sound packets)
- The attributes of the program such as the structure of the original images and the number of sound channels so the receiver can adapt the program to the characteristics of the receiver display and sound reproduction system

- Time information of the program to support recording or a scheduled reception

All of the required information can be supported by the DTTB transport syntax.

Conditional Access Identification

Conditional access systems can be supported by the DTTB transport syntax with bits identified in the packet header. Information about the conditional access mechanism, including key information, should be uniquely identified and carried as private data.

Picture Structure Information

Some Administrations interested in implementing DTTB services intend to provide a range of scalable services for use in different reception environments. Compressed and encoded image sequences may also serve as a format for program interchange. The ability of the video syntax to carry details of the picture sampling structure used in the coded image, including samples per line, lines per frame, frames per second, scanning format (interlace or progressive), and aspect ratio, facilitates use of the program material across a broad spectrum of applications.

Colorimetry

Information on the colorimetry characteristics of the coded video can be supported in the video sequence layer. This includes a description of the color primaries, transfer characteristics, and the color matrix coefficients, and allows the receiver appliance to properly accommodate image sequences derived from sources using different colorimetry.

Color Field Identification

Conventional television receivers will dominate the market at the start of DTTB services and will populate the market for many decades thereafter. The advantages of DTTB services may lead to a desire to make these services available to existing conventional receivers. Providing color field information in the video syntax helps the decoder reencode the image sequence for use by a conventional service-compatible output with reduced artifacts, particularly where the source images were derived from conventional program material.

Scene Changes and Local Program Insertion

Automatic scene change detection algorithms may be used by some coders to improve coding efficiency. Scene change information, when supplied by the original production facility, could prove useful to the video coder at both the compression and transport levels. The information could also prove useful to distribution systems to identify points in the data stream where switching between sources of transmitted bit streams could take place.

There is a further requirement to identify points in the transmitted bit stream where packet replacement can take place without noticeably disrupting the performance of the receiver. These are termed "clean-insertion" points and are useful where downstream (local, national, or regional) service providers wish to modify a cooperative or network service to accommodate it for local use. The DTTB system syntax provides for such a capability. In general, there are only certain fixed points in the elementary bit stream at which insertion is allowed. The local insertion point has to be a random entry point, but not all random entry points are suitable as insertion points.

Random entry into the video and audio application bit streams is necessary to support functions such as program switching. Random entry into an application is possible only if the coding for the elementary bit stream provides direct support of this function. A DTTB video bit stream might support random entry through the use of I-pictures (intraframe pictures that are coded without any prediction and, therefore, can be decoded without any prior information being present). The beginning of the video sequence header information for an I-picture could serve as a random entry point into a video elementary bit stream. In general, random entry points should also coincide with the start of a PES packet when they are used. The support for random entry at the transport layer comes from a flag in the adaptation header of the packet which indicates whether the packet does or does not contain a random entry point. The data payload of packets that constitute random access points must contain data that supports the random access point. This allows the discarding of packets directly at the transport layer when switching channels and searching for a resynchronization point in the transport bit stream. Generally, random access points should be provided as frequently as practicable to enable rapid channel switching at the receiver and efficient downstream access for local program insertion.

In addition to there being a random entry point available, the VBV_delay (video buffer verifier delay) needs to be at a certain system-defined level to allow clean local program insertions. The VBV_delay information can be computed and transmitted as part of the header data for a picture in the compressed video stream. This information defines how full the decoder video buffer needs to be before the bits of the current picture are extracted from the buffer, synchronizing the encoder and decoder processes. The VBV_delay information prevents buffer overflow or underflow.

The transport packet layer is also involved in local program insertions as the data stream splice points must be aligned. Implementation of the program insertion process is aided by using the splice_countdown field in the adaptation header. This field indicates ahead of time the number of packets until the packet where splicing and local program insertion is possible. The insertion of local programming also may result in a discontinuity of the PCR received at the decoder. Because this change in PCR is unexpected (changes in PCR values are usually expected only during program change), the decoder can lose synchronization. To prevent this from happening, information is transmitted in the adaptation header of the first packet after the splicing point to notify the decoder of the change of PCR values, allowing a change in the clock phase instead of a modification of the clock rate.

Field/Frame Rate and Film Pull-Down

Systems for use in the 60-Hz environment can be optimized for transmitting film-originated image sequences by transmitting the frame rate of the coded bit stream. This allows encoders to maximize coding efficiency by not transmitting redundant fields, and signals the decoder the proper order for displaying the decoded pictures. The DTTB frame rate syntax can be supported within the video sequence layer to support frame rates of 23.976 (24 ÷ 1.001), 24, 25, 29.97 (30 ÷ 1.001), 50, 59.94 (60 ÷ 1.001), and 60 Hz as well as providing extensions for future capabilities.

Pan and Scan

Receivers with 4:3 aspect ratio displays will dominate the market at the start of wide-screen (16:9) aspect ratio services and will populate the market for decades thereafter. The advantages of wide-screen DTTB services may lead to a desire to make these services available to existing analog-based receivers and other 4:3 aspect ratio display devices.

Pan and scan information could be transmitted as an extension of the picture layer syntax. The pan and scan extension would allow decoders to define a rectangular region which may be panned around the entire coded image and, thereby, identify a 4:3 aspect ratio window within a 16:9 coded image.

A FULLY FLEXIBLE TRANSPORT

The service multiplex and transport provides an efficient mechanism that allows the service provider with the flexibility to meet service demands. Each video, audio, and/or data service can be identified by a unique PID. The individual services that comprise a single program are identified by using the `program_map_table` to list the video, audio, and/or data PIDs associated with that program. Multiple programs can be combined into a single channel by listing the PIDs associated with the individual programs in the `program_association_table`. The system is made efficient through the use of flags, which allow those fields that are required to provide the information needed to process the service to be accessed. Fields that are not required have their flags set to zero, thereby releasing the data space for other use. New, as yet unidentified, services can be added at a later time by assigning them unique PIDs, thereby making the system extensible.

The information service multiplex and transport subsystem described above can provide the required foundation for the digital communication system. This subsystem takes the encoded elementary bit streams representing image data, sound data, and ancillary data, forms them into manageable packets of information, assigns an appropriate identification code to each packet, and multiplexes the packets into a single-transport bit stream that is flexible and extensible.

END NOTES

1. Chairman, ITU-R Task Group 11/3, "Proposed Revision to Chapter 3 of the Draft Report on Digital Terrestrial Television Broadcasting in the VHF/UHF bands," Doc. 11/3-14, 20 July 1994.

2. Chairman, ITU-R, Task Group 11/3, "Report of the Second Meeting of ITU-R Task Group 11/3, Geneva, 13–19 October 1993," 5 January 1994.

3. ITU-R Document TG11/3-87, "Service Transport Methods for Digital Terrestrial Television Broadcasting," 4 October 1994.

4. ATSC Document T3/258, "ATSC Digital Television Standard," 20 December 1994.

5. European Telecommunication Standard, Draft, prETS 300 429, "Digital Broadcasting Systems for Television, Sound, and Data Services; Framing Structure, Channel Coding and Modulation: Cable Systems, " August 1994.

6. ITU-R Document 11D/TEMP/10 (Rev. 1), Draft New Decision, "Navigation through a Multiplicity of TV Programmes," 19 October 1994.

7. ITU-R Document 11/39, Draft New Recommendation [11-3/XK], "Data Access Methods for Digital Terrestrial Television Broadcasting," 2 November 1994.

8. ITU-R Document 11D/TEMP/14, "Service and Programme Information Data for Digital Broadcasting Systems," 18 October 1994.

9. ITU Document 11/39, Draft New Recommendation [11-3/XK], "Data Access Methods for Digital Terrestrial Television Broadcasting," 2 November 1994.

10. ITU-R Document 11D/TEMP/10 (Rev. 1), Draft New Decision, "Navigate Through a Multiplicity of TV Programmes," 19 October 1994.

11. ITU-R Document 11D/TEMP14, "Service and Programme Information Data for Digital Broadcasting Systems," 18 October 1994.

4

Coding the Video Signal[1]

Given certain assumptions, it is possible to separate operations involv-
ing the generation of signals (the source) and consideration of the char-
acteristics of the transmission channel so that these two operations can
be dealt with and optimized independently. This is where the concepts
of separate source coding and channel coding arise. Source coding
exploits the inherent redundancy in the source signal to compress or
reduce the amount of data that needs to be transmitted, whereas chan-
nel coding provides mechanisms to protect that data. Data compression
may be lossless or it may introduce some degradation.

The ability to transport video services at reduced bit rates frees chan-
nel capacity for other services. This chapter provides an overview of
video compression technology.

INTRODUCTION

The digital terrestrial television broadcasting (DTTB)
system is designed to transmit high-quality video and
audio over a single 6-, 7-, or 8-MHz terrestrial channel.

Modern digital transmission technologies allow cable and fiber systems to deliver data at rates that exceed 10 Gbits/s. These technologies, however, when applied to the more constrained environment of wireless transmission deliver a maximum data service of between 17 and 24 Mbits/s within a single 6-, 7-, or 8-MHz terrestrial broadcasting channel.

A digitized high-definition television (HDTV) video source can generate information at a data rate of 1200–1500 Mbits/s. This implies a bit rate reduction by a factor of 50 or higher to allow an HDTV service to be transmitted in a terrestrial broadcasting channel. An examination of television images, however, shows that much of the information is redundant between points in any given picture and between points in adjacent pictures. To achieve the bit-rate reduction required, the DTTB system makes use of the total available channel capacity and exploits complex video compression techniques. The methods utilized may include source adaptive processing, motion estimation and compensation, transform representation, perceptual coding, and statistical coding (all of which are described in this chapter). In order to meet the requirements of the many applications and services envisioned, the DTTB system must accommodate both progressive and interlaced scanned pictures across a broad range of spatial and temporal resolutions. When the same techniques are applied to conventional television (525-line or 625-line) services, which typically require 1/5 the data rate of HDTV services, multiple program services can be supplied in a single broadcast channel.

VIDEO COMPRESSION BASICS

The objective in source coding image signals is to represent a video source with as few bits as possible while preserving the level of quality required for the given application. Video compression technology can be applied to provide efficient utilization of the available channel bandwidth for both video distribution and transmission systems and to reduce storage media requirements.

A basic block diagram of a typical digital video application is shown in Figure 4-1. The video source is encoded by the video encoder, and the output of the encoder is a string of bits that represents the video source. The channel coder transforms the string of bits to a form suitable for transmission over a communications channel through some form of modulation. The channel can represent wired or wireless transmission or a recording medium. The communication channel typically introduces some noise, and provision for error correction is made in the channel coder to compensate for this channel noise. At the receiver, the received signal is demodulated and transformed back into a string of bits by a channel decoder. The video decoder reconstructs the images from the string of bits for display.

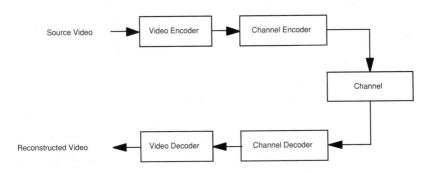

Figure 4-1. Video Processing.

A video encoder that provides compression capabilities consists of three basic operations, as shown in Figure 4-2. In the first stage, the video signal is analyzed and expressed in a more efficient *representation*, which facilitates the process of compression. An efficient representation concentrates most of the important information in a small number of values. If properly implemented, only this small fraction of the data needs to be transmitted for an appropriate reconstruction of the video signal.

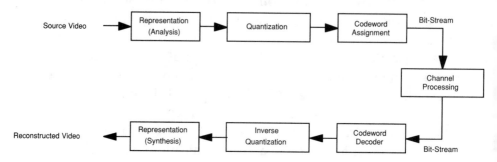

Figure 4-2. Video Compression System Overview.

Quantization, the second operation, determines the scaling (coarseness) of the represented data. The third operation provides assignment of *codewords*, which are strings of bits used to represent the data stream after quantization has occurred.

Each of the three operations is designed to exploit the redundancy (sameness in picture content) present in the video source, the limitations of the human visual system, and statistical properties of the data to reduce the number of bits required to reconstruct the original images. Removing the redundancy present in the video source deletes the repetition of the same or related information from the transmitted data stream. Exploiting the limitations of the human visual system deletes information in the video source that is not utilized by the human visual system. Taking advantage of the statistical properties of the data stream allows for more efficient transmission of the data.

Video can be considered as a sequence of pictures or frames. Intrapicture (intraframe) processing codes each picture based on the information contained within that picture only and removes only the spatial redundancy within a picture. Interpicture (interframe) processing codes each picture based on the information from that picture and adjacent pictures. Interpicture processing can be used to remove temporal redundancies within a sequence of images.

Standard Approaches

Differential pulse code modulation (DPCM) is one example of a compression algorithm. The process begins by sampling the picture in the horizontal and vertical dimensions, producing a rectangular array of picture elements called *pels*. A prediction of the luminance value of each pel can be generated from one or more previously coded pel values. The information actually transmitted is the difference between the predicted value and the actual intensity value of the pel. This difference is used to correct the value predicted in the receiver. The magnitude of each of the difference values tends to be much smaller than the actual pel value and results in a reduction in the transmitted data rate. DPCM schemes can be made adaptive in terms of the predictor or quantizer. One major advantage of DPCM coding is its simplicity. The DPCM approach works well at low compression ratios, such as in studio applications of television where high-quality, lossless transformations of images are required.

Transform coding is a mathematical process that alters the representation of the image from an array of pel values to an array of mathematical coefficients. Transform coding techniques attempt to utilize the correlation that exists among image pel values. The transform used often exploits the tendency in typical images to concentrate a large amount of energy in a small fraction of the transform coefficients and allows the rank ordering of coefficients in decreasing statistical significance. This is called the energy compaction property,[2] and the exploitation of this property makes it possible to code only a fraction of the transform coefficients without seriously affecting the image. One example of such a transform is the discrete cosine transform (DCT) in which the transform coefficients represent the spatial frequency components of the image. In DCT coding, an image is divided into many subimages or blocks (typically an 8 x 8 array of pels), and each block is coded separately. By coding one block at a time, the coder can adapt the algorithm to local image characteristics. For example, the method of choosing quantization and bit allocation methods may differ between uniform background regions and edge regions. The choice of which transform coefficients are to be coded depends on local image characteristics and can be controlled on the basis of system requirements. DCT coding is used in MPEG-2 and forms the basis of the proposed DTTB video source coding subsystem.

Subband transforms are another method of coding images. These transforms generally are computed by convolving the input signal with a set of bandpass filters and decimating (down-sampling) the results. Each decimated subband signal encodes a particular portion of the frequency spectrum. An adaptive bit allocation algorithm that distributes the bits among the subbands makes the subband coding scheme suitable for a wide variety of images.

In the *vector quantization* approach, the image sequence material is processed to yield a finite number of image vectors (similar to the image blocks used in transform coding). Properly selected, this finite set of vectors (called the vector **codebook**) can be used to reconstruct the original images with little degradation. Each image to be transmitted is described by a set of image vectors and the codebook is searched for a suitable match to each source vector. Compression is achieved by transmitting the vector address for the most similar image block rather than the image data.

Another method of reducing the information bit rate is the use of interframe coding. Interframe coding is used to obtain a higher compression rate than is achievable with intraframe coding alone by reducing the temporal redundancy between pictures. In interframe coding, a predicted frame is generated based on information from a previous and/or future frame, and the difference between the actual current frame and the predicted current frame (the residual) is coded. Motion prediction/compensation is used to estimate the current frame so as to make the residual as small as possible. This motion information is necessary to the recovery of the picture and must be coded and transmitted appropriately.

All of these methods can be used to code pictures. The encoded picture information along with the motion information is further compressed using variable-length coding to achieve maximum efficiency.

The steps to coding images, therefore, are as follows:

1. Formation of subimages for processing
2. Removal of temporal redundancy
3. Removal of spatial redundancy
4. Quantization of the results
5. Variable-length coding and codeword assignment.

Each of these steps and how they contribute to the reduction in the number of bits required to represent the images are described below.

FORMING THE SUBIMAGES FOR PROCESSING: THE VIDEO STRUCTURE HIERARCHY[3]

The first step in coding video is to organize the images into subimages or blocks for processing. The analog representation of television consists of lines of video and fields and frames of video. Analog video, therefore, is sampled in the vertical and temporal dimensions. Transforming the video into its digital representation requires sampling the video in the horizontal dimension. Each pel is, therefore, sampled in three dimensions: X (horizontal), Y (vertical), and T (time). Each pel consists of light intensity and color information quantized to an appropriate level of bits, usually of 8- or 10-bit accuracy.

The input video source to the DTTB video compression system is generally in the form of red (R), green (G), and blue (B) components matrixed into luminance (Y) and two color-difference (Cb and Cr) signals. Y corresponds to the luminance intensity (or black-and-white picture) and is equal to a prescribed mixture of the R, G, and B components. $Cr = Kr \bullet (R-Y)$ and $Cb = Kb \bullet (B-Y)$, where Kr and Kb are scaling coefficients. Use of three points of reference (R, G, B or Y, Cb, Cr) to represent the color space is termed a *tristimulous representation*.

The first coding step takes advantage of the characteristics of the human visual system to reduce the amount of information necessary to represent the luminance and color information in each pel. The human visual system responds differently to the luminance (Y) and chrominance (Cb, Cr) components. The human visual system is less sensitive to high-resolution information in the chrominance components than the high-resolution information in the luminance component. Matrixing the RGB components through a linear transformation into Y, Cb, Cr components reduces the correlation and exploits this difference in the human visual system. In a DTTB video compression system, the chrominance components may be low-pass filtered and subsampled along both the horizontal and vertical dimensions. Transporting the color-difference signals, for example, at one-half the horizontal and one-half the vertical resolution than the luminance information produces little noticeable degradation in the reconstructed visual display. MPEG system implementations take advantage of this factor to reduce the amount of data required for processing.

In the DTTB system, the pels are then organized into *blocks* for the purpose of further processing. A block normally consists of either an array of pel values or the transform of those pel values into an array of coefficients. A block represents a set of 8 x 8 values representing the luminance or chrominance information (see Figure 4-3).

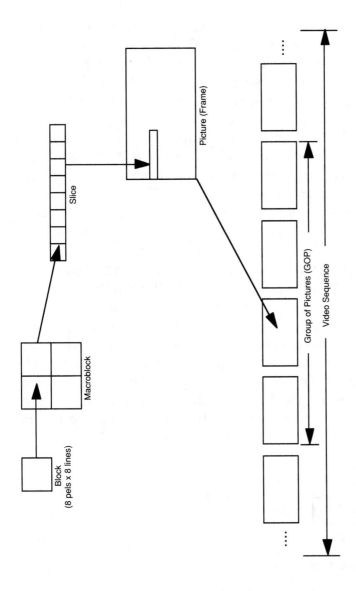

Figure 4-3. Video Structure Hierarchy.

Blocks of information can be organized into *macroblocks*. In the MPEG and DTTB systems, a macroblock consists of four blocks of luminance (Y) information (or a 16 x 16 array of values) and a number of chroma (Cr and Cb) blocks. When the number of chroma blocks is two (one each of the Cr and Cb blocks), as shown in Figure 4-4, a 4:2:0 chroma format is assumed. This means that the color information is transmitted at one-half the horizontal and one-half the vertical resolution of the luminance information.[4]

One or more contiguous macroblocks in a row are grouped together to form *slices*. The order of the macroblocks within a slice is the same as the conventional television raster scan being from left to right. Slices provide a convenient mechanism for the handling of errors. When an error occurs in the data stream, the decoder can move to the start of the next slice. The slice represents the minimum unit for recovery from and resynchronization after an error. The number of slices affects the efficiency of transfer; partitioning the data stream to have more slices provides for better error recovery but uses bits that could otherwise be used to improve picture quality.

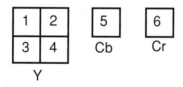

Figure 4-4. Macroblock Composition.

The primary coding unit of a video sequence is the individual video *frame* or *picture*. A video picture consists of the group of slices which constitute the active picture area.

One or more pictures (frames) in sequence are combined into a *group of pictures* (GOP) to allow random access into the sequence and to provide boundaries for interpicture coding.

Finally, a *video sequence* is represented by a *sequence header*, one or more groups of pictures, and an *end-of-sequence* code in the data stream.

REMOVAL OF TEMPORAL REDUNDANCY: MOTION ESTIMATION AND COMPENSATION

A video sequence is a series of still pictures shown in rapid succession to give the impression of continuous motion. The high frame rate necessary to achieve proper motion rendition usually results in much temporal redundancy (sameness in picture content) among the adjacent pictures. Motion compensation attempts to delete this temporal redundancy from the information that is transmitted.

Much of the variation in intensity from one picture to the next is due to object motion. In motion-compensated coding, the current picture is predicted from the previously encoded picture, estimating the motion between the two adjacent pictures and compensating for the motion. The difference between the current picture and the prediction of the current picture is called the motion-compensated residual. For a typical video sequence, the energy in the residual is much less than that in the original video due to the removal of the temporal redundancy. Encoding the residual rather than the video itself ensures that the temporally redundant information is not repeated. The motion estimation process assumes that the same imagery appears in consecutive video pictures, although possibly at different locations.

Although motion may be global throughout the picture or localized to a limited number of subimages (blocks) within the picture, system performance can be optimized by computing estimates of motion for each local block within the picture. The most common model for the local block motion is simple translational motion. This approach cannot represent the large number of possible motions, such as rotations, scale changes, and other complex motions. However, by assuming these motions only locally and by identifying and processing those blocks where the model fails separately by some other means, excellent performance can be achieved.

In this block-matching approach, the current picture, partitioned into blocks, is searched at the individual block level for the displacement that produces the "best match" among possible blocks in an adjacent frame. The process of block-matching motion-compensated prediction is illustrated in Figure 4-5. The difference between the current frame and its prediction is the motion-compensated residual or prediction error. The prediction error (difference signal) can be further compressed using the discrete cosine transform (DCT) to remove spatial correlation.

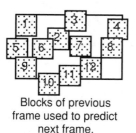

Blocks of previous
frame used to predict
next frame.

Frame after using
motion vectors to
adjust block positions.

Figure 4-5. Block of Reference Frame Used to Adjust Predicted Frame.

Multiple-prediction methods are available to provide motion compensation for progressive and interlaced pictures. The prediction methods include picture (frame) prediction, adaptive field prediction, a method termed "dual prime" (used for forward prediction only), and bidirectional prediction.

P-pictures are images where the prediction is in the forward direction only (i.e., predictions are formed only from pels in previously displayed pictures). Predicted pictures allow the exploitation of interframe coding techniques to improve the overall compression efficiency and picture quality.

Each macroblock within a P-picture can be either forward predicted or intraframe coded. If a macroblock is forward predicted, then either a frame-based or field-based prediction may be used. The decision is made by the encoder based on the smallest prediction error using each method. Regardless of whether field-based or frame-based prediction is used, the predicted macroblock is subtracted from the original macroblock, and only the "difference" values are encoded and transmitted.

A dual prime prediction mode has evolved which is an alternative "special" prediction mode based on field-based motion prediction. This mode can require fewer transmitted motion vectors than conventional field-based prediction.

Dual prime prediction averages field-based predictions of both fields in a macroblock predicted from the two nearest decoded fields in time. Each of the macroblock fields is predicted separately. In addition to the single field-based motion vector, a small "differential" vector (limited to vertical and horizontal component values of +1, 0, and -1) is also transmitted for each macroblock. Together, these vectors are used to calculate the pairs of motion vectors for a macroblock. The first prediction in the pair is simply the transmitted field-based motion vector. The second prediction vector is obtained by combining the differential vector with a scaled version of the first vector. Once both predictions are obtained, a single prediction for each macroblock field is calculated simply by averaging the two original predictions. The final averaged prediction is then subtracted from the macroblock field being encoded.[5]

The *B-picture* (bidirectional picture) prediction correlates the current picture with pictures which occur in the past and in the future. When a future picture is available to the decoder, a better prediction can be formed, thus saving bits and improving performance. B-picture prediction can be used for increasing the compression efficiency and perceived picture quality when encoding latency is not an important factor. It can be applied equally well to both interlaced and progressive scanned material. However, the use of B-pictures requires additional memory in the receiver. B-pictures are used because the increase in compression efficiency is noticeable, especially with progressive scanned sourced pictures.

It is understood that the B-pictures themselves cannot be used for predicting future pictures, and the use of B-pictures requires that the transmission order of pictures is different from the displayed order of pictures. Because the encoder and decoder must reorder the video frames, the total latency of the process is increased. In the example illustrated in Figure 4-6, there is one B-picture between each pair of I/P-pictures (intraframe/predicted pictures), and each picture is labeled with both its display order and transmission order. Although a B-picture is displayed between its adjacent I/P-pictures, it is transmitted out of sequence. This is so that the video decoder has the adjacent pictures decoded and available for prediction.

For a given macroblock within the B-picture, the encoder has four options for its prediction. They are forward prediction, backward prediction, bidirectional prediction, and intraframe coding. When bidirectional prediction is used, the forward and backward predictors are averaged and then subtracted from the target macroblock to form the prediction error. The prediction error is then transformed, quantized, and transmitted in the usual manner. The dual prime and bidirectional methods are complementary, as the dual prime mode is used for interlaced image sequences only and is precluded when a sequence uses bidirectional frames.

Figure 4-6 illustrates a time sequence of video frames consisting of intracoded pictures (referred to as I-pictures); predictive coded pictures ("P-pictures"); and bidirectionally predictive coded pictures ("B-pictures").

P-pictures are predicted using the most recently encoded P-picture or I-picture in the sequence. In Figure 4-6, P-pictures occur every second frame except when an I-picture is used.

The MPEG syntax allows the choice of the frequency of occurrence of I-pictures to be selected at the encoder. This allows consideration of the need for random access and the location of scene cuts in the video sequence. The choice of number of bidirectional pictures between any pair of reference (I- or P-) pictures can also be determined at the encoder.

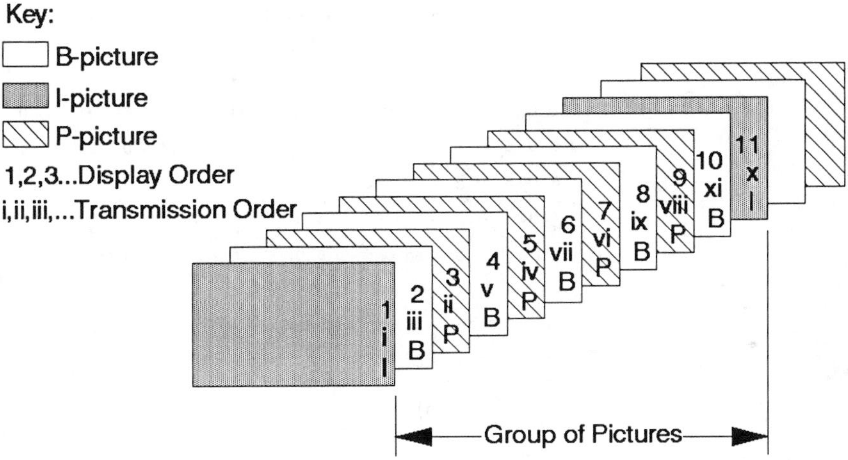

Key:

B-picture

I-picture

P-picture

1,2,3...Display Order

i,ii,iii,...Transmission Order

Group of Pictures

Figure 4-6. Video Frame Order.

Motion compensation is a form of predictive coding applied along the temporal dimension. For typical video pictures produced as progressively scanned frames, prediction by motion compensation produces more than adequate results. For some pictures, such as those at scene changes, however, the resulting prediction is not as good. Even within a given picture, some regions may be predicted well with motion compensation, whereas other regions may not be predicted very well using motion compensation based on translational motion. In some cases, therefore, the system may perform worse with predictive coding than by simply coding the picture itself.

REMOVAL OF SPATIAL INFORMATION REDUNDANCY: THE DISCRETE COSINE TRANSFORM

Motion compensation reduces the temporal redundancy of the video signal, but there still remains spatial redundancy in the motion-compensated residual. In the special case where no motion-compensated processing is performed, the only opportunity to reduce the data rate is to encode the original pictures as a series of I-pictures.

DCT-DC Component ⟶

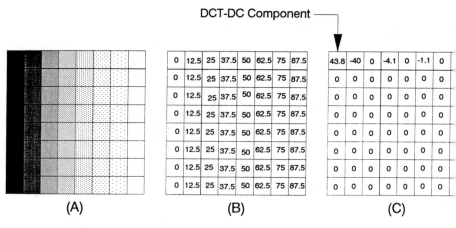

(A)   (B)   (C)

Figure 4-7. Discrete Cosine Transform.

As shown in Figure 4-7, the 8 x 8 blocks of spatial intensity showing variations of luminance and chrominance pel information is converted into 8 x 8 arrays of coefficients relating to the spatial frequency content of the original intensity information.[6]

In Figure 4-7A, an 8 x 8 pel array representing, perhaps, the edge of a black to white transition is shown as a gray scale. In Figure 4-7B, the gray scale has been digitized and is represented by its pel intensity amplitude numerical values. In Figure 4-7C, the gray-scale block is represented by its frequency transformation coefficients, appropriately quantized. The (0, 0) average value is a 9-bit number, while the three remaining values are shown as 8-bit, signed values. The discrete cosine transform (DCT) compacts most of the energy of the residual into only a small fraction of the transform coefficients. The coding and transmission of only these high-energy coefficients can result in the reconstruction of high-quality video. The DCT has good energy-compaction properties. The DCT of a two-dimensional signal may be computed by applying the one-dimensional DCT separately first to the rows and then to the columns of the signal. The most important coefficient resides in array position (0, 0) and represents the DC coefficient or average value of the array. The partitioning of the residual into small blocks before taking the transform not only allows spatially adaptive processing but also reduces the computational and memory requirements.

The transform process does not reduce the number of bits required to represent the image, as the number of coefficients required to represent the block is the same as the number necessary to represent the array of pels. However, the transform coefficients lend themselves to further processing, such as quantizing the coefficients or run-length coding of the "0s" that are suitable for bit-rate reduction. By exploiting the spatial frequency properties of the human visual system, the DCT coefficients can be encoded to match the human visual system so that only the perceptually important DCT coefficients are encoded and transmitted.

QUANTIZING THE COEFFICIENTS

The processing discussed up to this point has created a representation in the form of motion vectors and spatial frequency coefficients of the original luminance and chrominance components of the pictures. However, no compression has been achieved. Most of the perceptually important information has been compressed into only a fraction of these "pieces of information," and these data can be selected and encoded for transmission.

The goal of video compression is to maximize the video quality for a given bit rate. This requires distribution of the limited number of available bits to the more important representation factors. Quantization is a process of dividing the coefficients by a value of N, which is greater than 1, and rounding the answer to the nearest integer value. Quantization is performed to scale the values and thus reduce the actual bit rate required. The quantization process is a lossy step in the compression algorithm because some information is permanently lost.

The human eye is less sensitive to high-resolution detail; therefore, the high frequency DCT coefficients can be more heavily scaled (coarsely coded) and the resulting errors will not be perceptible. The differing perceptual importance of the various coefficients can be exploited by "allocating the bits" to shape the quantization error (known as quantization noise) into the perceptually less important areas. For example, low spatial frequency coefficients may be quantized finely, whereas the high-frequency coefficients, which may have less statistical significance, may be quantized more coarsely. A simple method to achieve different step sizes is to normalize or weight each coefficient based on its visual importance. All of the normalized coefficients may then be quantized in the same manner, such as rounding to the nearest integer. The quantizer may also include a dead zone (enlarged interval around zero) to quantize or core to zero small noiselike perturbations of the element value, as shown in Figure 4-8. The MPEG and DTTB standards allow for changing the quantization values for each block when required for the coding of complex pictures.

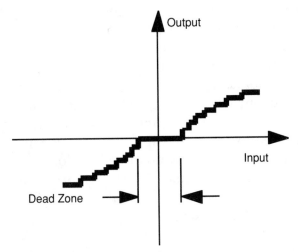

Figure 4-8. Variable Quantization.

MPEG-2 syntax allows the quantization matrices to be specified for every picture for improved coding efficiency, and the quantization matrices can be adjusted to help match the distribution of the data to the channel data rate. Transmitting the quantizer matrices adds bits to the compressed data stream. If sent every picture in the progressive mode, the matrices could consume approximately 0.1% of the channel bandwidth. This modest amount of overhead can be reduced by updating the quantization matrix at the start of each GOP or when the difference between the desired quantizer matrix and the prevailing quantizer matrix becomes significant.

VARIABLE-LENGTH CODING AND CODEWORD ASSIGNMENT

Quantization creates an efficient discrete representation of the data to be transmitted. The quantized values can be represented using uniform or fixed-length codewords. Every quantized value will then be represented by the same number of bits. Greater efficiency, in terms of bit rate, can be achieved by employing what is known as *entropy coding*. Entropy coding attempts to exploit the statistical properties of the signal to be encoded. A signal, whether it is a pel value or a transform coefficient, has a certain amount of information, or entropy, based on the probability of the different possible values or events occurring. By realizing that some events occur more frequently than others, the average bit rate may be reduced. It is possible to assign a shorter codeword to those values occurring frequently and a longer one to those occurring less frequently. The Morse code is an example of an entropy coded data system with fewer "bits" (dots and dashes) used to represent the letter "E," which occurs often in the English language, than are used to represent the letter "Q," which appears relatively infrequently.

From information theory, the entropy is the theoretically minimum possible average bit rate required in coding a message. One optimal codeword design method, simple to use, and which results in lowering the average bit rate, is Huffman coding, a method of variable-length coding.

In Huffman coding, a code book is generated which minimizes the entropy, subject to the codeword constraints of integer lengths and unique decodability. Events which are more likely to occur are assigned shorter-length codewords, whereas those which are less likely to occur are assigned longer-length codewords. Huffman coding results in the average bit rate being reduced. The generation of the code book is achieved by using a representative set of data to estimate the probability of each event. Optimal performance can be achieved by designing an individual code book for each element to be encoded. However, this results in a large number of code books. Close to optimal performance is achieved by using a new code book where elements with similar statistics are grouped and encoded together. Similarly, the size of each code book can be reduced by grouping together very unlikely events into a single entry within the book. When any event belonging to this group occurs, the codeword for the group is transmitted followed by an exact description of the event.

When the transform/subband coefficients are properly scanned, the coefficients tend to be ordered from high amplitude to low amplitude, with the result that zero-value coefficients typically appear as a single long run which can be coded by a short codeword. There may be a few nonzero low-frequency coefficients and a sparse scattering of nonzero high-frequency coefficients, but in most cases, the great majority of coefficients will have been quantized to zero, particularly where the array represents the residual of prediction errors. To exploit this phenomenon, the two-dimensional array of transform coefficients may be reformatted and prioritized into a one-dimensional sequence through zigzag (see Figure 4-9) or some alternate similar structured scanning. This results in most of the important nonzero coefficients (in terms of energy and visual perception) being grouped together early in the sequence. They will be followed by long runs of coefficients that are quantized to zero. These zero-valued coefficients can be efficiently represented through run-length encoding. In run-length encoding, the number of consecutive zero coefficients (the run) before a nonzero coefficient is encoded, followed by the nonzero coefficient value. The run length and the coefficient value can be entropy coded, either separately or jointly. The scanning pattern separates most of the zero and the nonzero coefficients into groups, thereby enhancing the efficiency of the run-length encoding process. Also, a special *end-of-block* (EOB) marker may be used to signify when all of the remaining coefficients in the sequence are equal to zero.

There are two important issues that arise when considering the application of entropy coding. First, entropy coding involves increased complexity and memory requirements over fixed-length codes. Second, entropy coding coupled with the variations which occur in the video signal results in a time-varying bit rate. A buffer control mechanism is necessary when the variable bit-rate source coder is to be coupled with the constant bit-rate channel associated with the DTTB system or recording media.

DC-Component

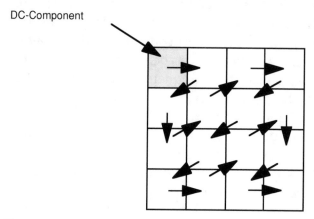

Figure 4-9. Zigzag Scanning Pattern.

BUFFER

Motion compensation, adaptive quantization, and variable-length coding produce highly variable amounts of compressed video data as a function of time. For example, the compressed bit rate after a scene change can be several times greater than the bit rate of the channel. A buffer is used to regulate the variable-input bit rate into a fixed-output bit rate for transmission. The state of the buffer is calculated periodically and relayed back to a rate controller that adjusts the quantization level. Buffer size is constrained by the maximum tolerable delay through the system and by cost. The fullness of the buffer is controlled by adjusting the amount of allowable distortion or quantization error in each image block. In the encoder, the buffer will fill more quickly if the distortion is low. If the bit rate decreases significantly, a finer quantization can be performed to increase it.

Conversely, when the buffer approaches an overflow state, making the quantization coarser (increasing the distortion), this lowers the bit rate. A feedback control system regulates the quantization/distortion level which controls the buffer fullness to prevent underflow or overflow.

The visibility of distortion due to an increase in scene complexity is minimized by smoothly adjusting the quantization level. This is facilitated by accurately modeling the rate versus distortion level, because an accurate model allows the desired buffer fullness to be achieved for each frame. The model allows an estimate of complexity to be translated into a bit rate for a given frame.

MPEG-2 LEVELS AND PROFILES[7]

The MPEG syntax addresses a variety of performance grades. These different grades provide for differing levels of performance and complexity and are described in a matrix of **Profiles** and **Levels**. The matrix is described in Table 4-1. A *profile* is a defined subset of the entire MPEG syntax. A *level* is defined set of constraints imposed on parameters in the bit stream. The constraints may include limits on the values of the parameters, such as limits on the structure and output data rate that the encoder can process. To be MPEG compliant means that a given coder will work at its own (or lower) level and profile.

The MPEG-2 coding systems are mainly intended for distribution applications. The suitability of the existing MPEG-2 video coding profiles and levels to studio and contribution applications is under study. Some specific features under consideration are as follows:[8]

- The use of chrominance subsampling (4:2:0 format) may have a significant impact on the quality after some kinds of postprocessing (as chroma-key), and a profile/level employing a 4:2:2 format may be more appropriate.

- The use of bidirectional prediction for some frames (B-frames) may have an influence on the quality after slow motion or after cascading several codes.
- Field- or frame-based editing needs to be supported.
- Programs are processed using a production switcher with video effects that may provide for geometric expansion, reduction, rotation, and other forms of distortion, and a level appropriate to this application needs to be identified.
- Trick mode operation (frozen pictures, slow motion, quick motion) needs to be supported.

The philosophy behind the MPEG-2 syntax structure is the intent to define for each profile and level certain functionalities from the large but limited set of functionalities provided as syntax elements. As one moves from low profiles and levels to higher profiles and levels, increasingly more functionalities are provided. Higher profile/level decoders can decode signals in the same profile but lower level or the same level but lower profile. This capability suggests the use of a standard decoder at as high a profile and level as possible. Since the encoding can be done at a lower functionality than the receiver decoder, the service provider has the freedom to provide services at different qualities and functionalities without being constrained by receiver capabilities. The generally held view suggests that the standard allow for improvements and evolution in the future and not be constrained by short-term concerns. It is this philosophy that forms the basis for the DTTB standard.[9]

Table 4-1. MPEG Levels and Profiles

	Simple Profile	Main Profile	SNR Scalable Profile	Spatially Scalable Profile	High Profile
	I-Frames P-Frames B-Frames 4:2:0 Non-scalable	I-Frames P-Frames B-Frames 4:2:0 Non-scalable	I-Frames P-Frames B-Frames 4:2:0 SNR scalable	I-Frames P-Frames B-Frames 4:2:0 SNR scalable Spatially scalable	I-Frames P-Frames B-Frames 4:2:0 4:2:2 SNR scalable Spatially scalable
High Level ≤ 1920 pels ≤ 1152 lines		≤ 80 Mbits/s			≤ 100 Mbits/s
High-1440 Level ≤ 1440 pels ≤ 1152 lines		≤ 60 Mbits/s		≤ 60 Mbits/s	≤ 80 Mbits/s
Main Level ≤ 720 pels ≤ 576 lines	≤ 15 Mbits/s	≤ 15 Mbits/s	≤ 15 Mbits/s		≤ 20 Mbits/s
Low Level ≤ 352 pels ≤ 288 Lines		≤ 4 Mbits/s	≤ 4 Mbits/s		

Notes:

1. Within the matrix, only profile/level combinations showing maximum data rate are defined compliance points.
2. Decoders defined for a specified compliance point (profile and layer) shall be capable of accommodating images encoded at lower-order compliance points.
3. In the SNR scalable, spatially scalable, and high profiles, a maximum of one SNR enhancement layer is allowed in addition to the base layer.
4. In the spatially scalable and high profiles, a maximum of one spatially scalable enhancement layer is allowed in addition to the base layer and SNR enhancement layer.

IMAGE REFRESHING

A coding algorithm based on motion-compensated prediction is not practical without some form of image refreshing. This refreshing may be constant or variable and periodic.

In the case of coding of a still image, which is replicated at video frame rates, the motion vectors and the prediction error would be zero. If the decoder were started with a sequence of zero prediction frames, as happens during a channel change, then a blank or zero reconstructed image would result. If the viewer changed to a channel transmitting a coded still image, the still image would never appear. A portion of the original picture must be spatially or temporally mixed with the prediction in the encoder to allow the decoder to synchronize to the encoder after decoder initialization.

Two different mechanisms have been identified for refreshing. I-frame refreshing uses periodic intracoded frames. The advantages are that it provides clean insertion points in the compressed bit stream and nominal picture quality after acquisition (typically controlled to be 0.5 s). The disadvantages are that it requires a larger bit buffer, it increases latency, and it complicates rate control.

Progressive refreshing uses periodic intracoded macroblocks or slices. The advantages over I-frame refreshing are that it reduces the required buffer size, it simplifies rate control, and it reduces latency. One disadvantage is that motion vectors must be restricted in order to guarantee complete picture buildup after channel acquisition or channel errors.

PROCESSING OF INTERLACED IMAGES

There are two options when processing interlaced video signals. The first option is to separate each picture into its two field components and then process the two fields independently (Figure 4-10). The second option is to process the two fields as a single frame by interleaving the lines of field 1 and field 2 (Figure 4-11).

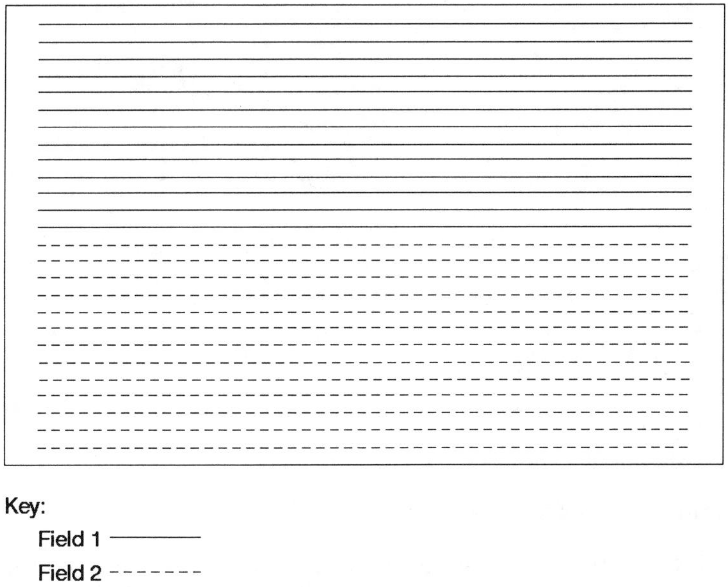

Key:
    Field 1 ————————
    Field 2 - - - - - - -

Figure 4-10. Field Processing.

Frame processing works better than field processing when there is little or no motion between fields. Because each frame has twice as many lines or samples for a given picture height, there will be more correlation between samples, resulting in a more efficient compression. Therefore, to achieve the same accuracy, field processing will require a higher bit rate or, alternatively, for equal bit rates, frame processing will achieve greater accuracy. Similar advantages over field processing will be realized if horizontally moving features have little horizontal detail or if vertically moving features have little vertical detail. In other regions, where there is little detail of any sort, frame processing may still work better than field processing, no matter how rapidly changes occur.

Key:

　　Field 1 ————

　　Field 2 - - - - - -

Figure 4-11. Frame Processing.

Field processing generally works better than frame processing in detailed moving areas. In such cases, the interleaving of the first and second fields would introduce spurious high vertical frequencies if frame processing were used. This would reduce the correlation between lines and, therefore, the effectiveness of the compression process.

Digital terrestrial television broadcasting (DTTB) system implementation may combine the advantages of both frame processing and field processing by adaptively selecting one of the two modes on a block-by-block basis. The mode which is selected is the one which maximizes correlation between adjacent lines within the block. Because the decision is made on a local basis, the system can adjust to scenes containing both moving and nonmoving features, and, therefore, accurately produce vertical details in nonmoving areas and deliver good motion rendition in others.

PERCEPTUAL WEIGHTING: COEFFICIENT SELECTION BY PERCEPTUAL SENSITIVITY

As discussed earlier, the human visual system is not uniformly sensitive to the distortions or errors in reconstructed images due to quantization of the DCT coefficients. The amount of visible distortion resulting from quantization error for a given coefficient depends on the frequency associated with the coefficient number, the local brightness in the original image, and the duration or the temporal characteristic of the error.

Displays and human visual systems exhibit nonuniform sensitivity to detail as a function of local average brightness. Loss of detail in dark areas of the picture is not as visible as it is in brighter areas. High-frequency coefficient error is much less visible in textured areas of the picture than in relatively flat areas. Distortions are easily masked when their duration is one or two frames and provides an effective mechanism after scene changes where the first frame or two can be greatly distorted without being perceptibly annoying.

A DCT DC-coefficient (0, 0) error results in average value distortion of the corresponding block of pels, which can expose block boundaries. This is more visible than higher-frequency coefficient errors, which appear as noise or texture.

In most instances, a given coefficient is transmitted whenever its quantized error is nonzero. However, selecting some nonzero coefficients for elimination allows a fine level of quantization to be applied to the remaining coefficients, potentially improving the overall picture. Perceptual selection uses the properties of the human visual system to code pictures using fewer bits within a perceptually consistent level of quality. For each transform block, the perceptual selection method determines the acceptable amount of distortion allowed in each frequency band. If the magnitude of a coefficient is smaller than the acceptable distortion level, then the coefficient is set to zero, regardless of the quantization step size level.

FILM MODE

Digital terrestrial television broadcasting (DTTB) systems developed for use in 60-Hz environments may include an ability to detect source material originating from 24-fps (frames per second) film that has been converted to 60 fps using the 3:2 pull-down process. Due to the 3:2 pull-down method, some fields are known to be identical. The DTTB system can detect this redundancy through utilization of a film detection method that looks for the 3:2 pull-down pattern. When the film mode is detected, the system could then remove the redundancy and convert it back to the original 24-fps source format prior to video encoding. The removal of redundancy ensures that the same information is not transmitted repeatedly, thus significantly improving the efficiency of the video compression system.

The system may also be able to detect 25- or 30-fps material that has been converted to a 50- or 60-fps progressive scan format by simple frame repetition. When this conversion is detected, the encoder will discard the redundant frame and indicate to the decoder that each frame is to be displayed twice.

TRANSPORTING THE VIDEO BIT STREAM

The final step is to form the compressed video bit stream into packets and transport the information to the receiver. The video bit stream is preceded by a sequence header, information describing the format of the sequence, the picture data, and an `end_of_sequence_code`. The video bit stream sequence header is shown in Figure 4-12 and described in Table 4-2.

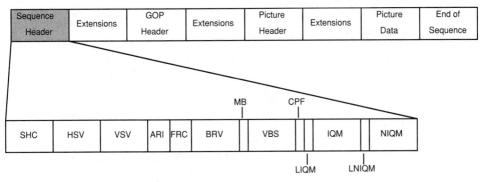

Figure 4-12. Video Bit Stream Format.

The sequence header extensions provide profile and level information, source video and scanning format, source chroma resolution and color primaries information, source opto-electronic transfer characteristics, and the size extensions described in Table 4-2.

Table 4-2. Video Bit Stream Sequence Header.

Function	Usage
SHC	32-bit `sequence_header_code`: (0000 01B3) identifies beginning of sequence header.
HSV	12-bit `horizontal_size_value`: `horizontal_size` is a 14-bit integer; 12 least significant bits are defined in HSV, 2 most significant bits are defined in `horizontal_size_extension`.
VSV	12-bit `vertical_size_value`: `vertical_size` is a 14-bit integer; 12 least significant bits are defined in VSV, 2 most significant bits are defined in `vertical_size_extension`.
ARI	4-bit `aspect_ratio_information`: 0 = forbidden, 1 = square pixels, 2 = 4:3 display ARI, 3 = 16:9 display ARI, 4–F are reserved.
FRC	4-bit `frame_rate_code`: 0 = forbidden, 1 = 23.976 (24 ÷ 1.001), 2 = 24, 3 = 25, 4 = 29.97 (30 ÷ 1.001), 5 = 30, 6 = 50, 7 = 59.94 (60 ÷ 1.001), 8 = 60, 9–F are reserved.

Table 4-2. (continued)

Function	Usage
BRV	18-bit b i t_r a t e_v a l u e : 18 least significant bits of bit rate; 12 most significant bits are in b i t_r a t e_e x t e n s i o n; 3FFF FFFF implies variable bit rate.
MB	1-bit m a r k e r_b i t = 1.
VBS	10-bit v b v_b u f f e r_s i z e : 10 least significant bits of buffer size; 8 most significant bits are in v b v_b u f f e r_s i z e_e x t e n s i o n; stipulates buffer size needed to decode sequence with B = 16•1024•v b v_b u f f e r_s i z e.
CPF	1-bit c o n s t r a i n e d_p a r a m e t e r_f l a g = 0 (used in MPEG-1).
LIQM	1-bit l o a d_i n t r a_q u a n t i z e r_f l a g: when set to 1, indicates IQM follows; when set to 0, indicates no change in values.
IQM	8•64-bit i n t r a_q u a n t i z e r_m a t r i x : a list of 64, 8-bit unsigned integers.
LNIQM	1-bit l o a d_n o n_i n t r a_q u a n t i z e r_f l a g: when set to 1, indicates NIQM follows; when set to 0, indicates no change in values.
NIQM	8•64-bit n o n_i n t r a_q u a n t i z e r_m a t r i x : a list of 64, 8-bit unsigned integers.

The GOP Header provides time code information and B-picture flags.

The Picture Header describes the type of picture coding (I-picture, P-picture, B-picture), v b v_d e l a y, and spaces for flags. The Picture Header Extension provides picture structure and precision information.

The s e q u e n c e_e n d_c o d e (0000 01B7) terminates the video sequence.

END NOTES

1. ITU-R Document 11-3/10, "Digital Terrestrial Television Broadcasting in the VHF/UHF Bands: Video Compression Technology Overview," 6 June 1994.

2. D. Pearson, ed., *Image Processing*, McGraw-Hill Book Company, New York, 1991, p. 208.

3. ISO/IEC IS 13818-2, International Standard, Video.

4. When the number of chroma blocks is four (two each of the Cr and Cb blocks), a 4:2:2 chroma format is assumed. When the number of chroma blocks is eight (four each of the Cr and Cb blocks), a 4:4:4 chroma format is assumed. In this latter case, the color information is transmitted at the same horizontal and vertical resolution as the luminance information.

5. ATSC Document T3/259, "Guide to the Use of the ATSC Digital Television Standard," 9 August 1994.

6. ITU-R Document 11-3/15, "MPEG Digital Compression Systems," 9 August 1994.

7. ISO/IEC IS 13818-2, International Standard, MPEG Video.

8. ITU Document 11B/TEMP/34, "Study of Requirements for a New MPEG Profile for the Broadcast Studio Application," 20 October 1994.

9. ITU Document 11/40, Draft New Recommendation [11-3/XL], "Videocoding for Digital Terrestrial Television Broadcasting," 2 November 1994.

5

Coding the
Audio Signal

Significant progress has been made over the past decade in bit-rate reduction encoding of digitized audio signals. A stereo sound (left, right) signal pair, each sampled at the nominal AES/EBU[1] rate of 48 kHz and at 16–20 bits per channel, produces a bit stream of between 1.536 and 1.920 Mbits/s. Currently envisioned, surround-sound services include six channels (or 5.1 channels),[2] implying a data stream with a total bit rate in excess of 4.6 Mbits/s.

Digital audio compression technology developed prior to 1990 reduced requirements of a single-channel sound service from 1.536 Mbits/s to 128–156 kbits/s. The techniques used employ complex envelope coding and adaptive bit allocation and take advantage of the frequency and temporal masking properties of the human hearing process. Improvements in compression technology as applied to multichannel services have been developed which allow a six-channel service to be transmitted at 384 kbits/s, a reduction in bit rate of 12:1. The more advanced approach takes advantage of the statistical redundancy existing in multichannel services.

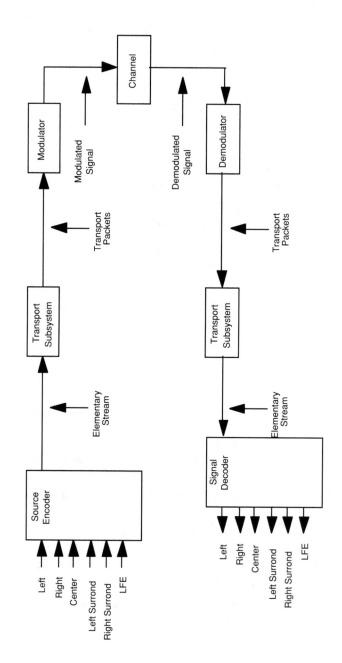

Figure 5-1. Audio Service Block Diagram.

INTRODUCTION

One goal of a communications system is to carry sound signals presented at the input to the system with sufficient accuracy to allow the receiver to reproduce those signals at the output in a manner that recreates the original sound. The amount of information required to represent the sound signals may be reduced in order to utilize the broadcast or recording media efficiently. A generic audio transport system is shown in Figure 5-1. In the example shown, the input audio is presented in the form of six separate channels representing a surround-sound service. The example shown also assumes that each of the channels is represented by a digital pulse code modulation (PCM) data stream. In any digital audio system, the output of the **source encoder** is a string of bits that represents the sound source. The **transport subsystem** formats that bit stream for presentation to the modulator. The transport subsystem allows multiple audio channels and services to be multiplexed into a single transmission channel by dividing each audio elementary bit stream into packets of data, attaching a packet header that describes the contents of the packet. The packets can then be time multiplexed into a single bit stream limited only by the capacity of the bit stream. The **modulator** includes a channel coder subsystem which transforms the bit stream to a form suitable for transmission over the channel. The channel can represent wired or wireless transmission or a recording medium. The communication channel typically introduces some noise, and provision for error correction is made in the channel coder to compensate for this channel noise.

At the demodulator, the received signal is demodulated and transformed back into a string of bits by a channel decoder. The audio signal decoder reconstructs the original individual sound channels from the string of bits.

The amount of digital information needed to accurately reproduce the original sound service may be reduced by applying a compression algorithm resulting in a reduction in the amount of information which must be transmitted or recorded.[3]

GENERIC SYSTEM DESCRIPTION

The digital compression algorithm attempts to represent original sound service using fewer bits than required by the PCM data stream. Any reduction of bits introduces errors. The challenge in providing a bit-rate reduced sound service is to code the signal in a manner in which the errors that are introduced are inaudible to humans.

Two mechanisms are available for reducing the bit rate of sound signals. The first utilizes statistical correlation to remove redundancy from the signal stream. The second uses the psychoacoustical characteristics of the human hearing system such as spectral and temporal masking to reduce the number of bits required to recreate the original sounds.

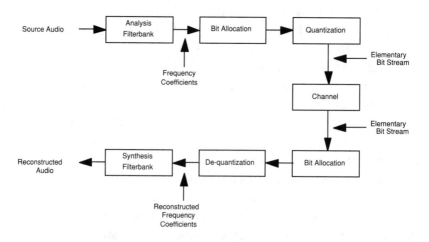

Figure 5-2. Generic System Block Diagram.

Two systems, the MPEG-2 and AC-3 systems, have been deemed appropriate for use in the DTTB environment. Both systems use a frequency domain representation of the audio channel in order to take advantage of the frequency-masking properties of the human hearing system. A generic block diagram is shown in Figure 5-2. In each application, the frequency spectrum of the source audio is separated into subbands by the use of a subband or a time/frequency mapping transform filter bank (**analysis filter bank**). This results in representation of the audio signal as a set of narrowbands of frequencies. The output of the transform or filter bank is used to calculate a time-dependent masking threshold using a specific psychoacoustic model. The subband samples are quantized and coded with the quantization levels selected to keep the noise level introduced by quantizing below the masking threshold. This quantizing mechanism establishes the number of bits allocated (**bit allocator**) to the samples. There are two approaches to bit allocation: forward adaptive and backward adaptive.

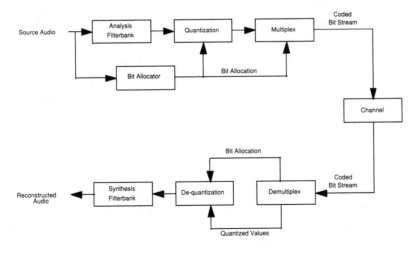

Figure 5-3. Forward Adaptive Bit Allocation.

Forward adaptive bit allocation (see Figure 5-3) implies that the *encoder* calculates the bit allocation and explicitly codes the allocation into the bit stream. This method should produce the most accurate allocation because the encoder has access to the complete input signal. The encoder calculates the optimum bit allocation within the limits of the psychoacoustic (frequency-masking) model employed. Another feature of this approach is that the model may be changed at any time without impacting the installed base of receivers, as the psychoacoustic model is resident only in the encoder and is communicated to the decoder. The primary disadvantage in using this approach is the need to allocate a portion of the available data capacity of the channel to deliver the bit allocation model to the decoder. For instance, the IEC/ISO MPEG-1 layer II audio encoder uses a data rate of nearly 4 kbits/s per channel to transmit the bit allocation model based on a time resolution of 24 ms and frequency resolution of 750 Hz. When the signal spectrum contains spectral lines in every 750-Hz frequency band, all bands have to be allocated bits and very limited bit-rate reduction would be obtained before audible artifacts would occur. The use of a finer frequency grid may produce a spectral density pattern that allows bits to be removed between spectral lines, but the improvement in the frequency resolution requires a linear increase in the allocation data rate (an increase by a factor of N to improve the frequency resolution by a factor of N).

The backward adaptive bit allocation technique (see Figure 5-4) depends on the spectral envelope of the coded audio data for the creation of the bit allocation without explicit information from the encoder. This means that none of the capacity of the data channel needs to be assigned to this function and all bits are available for coding audio. Backward adaptive systems trade efficiency in use of the data channel for possible increases in error of reconstruction, because the bit allocation is computed in the decoder from information

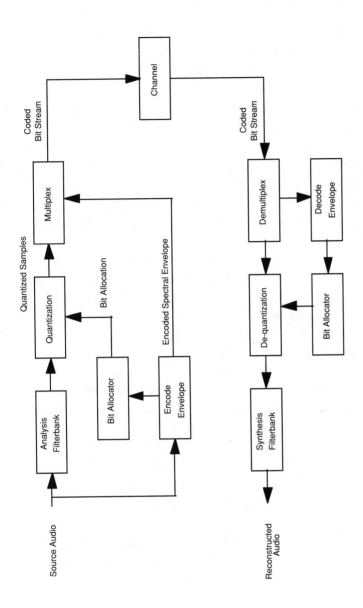

Figure 5-4. Backward Adaptive Bit Allocation.

contained in the bit stream that may be of limited accuracy. By allocating bits in the decoder, the complexity and cost of the decoder is increased, which is contrary to the desire to keep decoder costs low. System extensibility is also affected because the bit allocation algorithm available at the encoder must be fixed once decoders are deployed in the field.

Regardless of the model, the function of the analysis filter bank in the encoder is to change the representation of the audio signal from the time domain into the frequency domain, resulting in a set of coefficients that represent the spectral content of the audio signal. The function of the synthesis filter bank in the decoder is to reverse that process. The frequency domain is the more efficient domain for performing psychoacoustic-based audio compression. The configurations of the analysis and synthesis filter banks are constrained by trade-offs among frequency resolution, time resolution, and cost. Steady-state audio signals benefit from finer frequency resolution, and transient signals benefit from finer time resolution. Finer frequency resolution requires longer blocks of audio which must be buffered. Finer time resolution also increases the amount of random access memory (RAM) required to support the process. The increased RAM and associated multiply/accumulate arithmetic cycles during the transform process result in higher costs.

The individual transform frequency coefficients are usually coded into a binary floating-point notation (an exponent and a mantissa). The transforms are scaled so that all values are smaller than 1.0. An example of a binary value to 20-bit precision might be 0.0000 0000 0010 1010 1110_2. In this example, the leading number of zeros in the coefficient equals 10 (binary 1010) and represents the exponent or **scale factor** in multiples of 6 dB. Scale factors with resolution finer than 6 dB are employed by some systems. The value is left-shifted by the coefficient and the value to the right of the decimal point (10 1010

1110) is the mantissa, which is coarsely quantized. The use of exponents allows the system to accommodate a wide dynamic range. The mantissa is coded with a limited precision, which results in quantizing noise. The synthesis filter bank in the decoder constrains the quantizing noise to be nearly the same frequency as the quantized signal. The frequency domain coefficients may be coarsely quantized because the resulting noise, being nearly the same frequency as the audio signal, is rendered subjectively inaudible due to the psychoacoustic masking phenomena. The entire set of coded exponents forms a representation of the overall signal spectrum and is referred to as the spectral envelope. The bit allocation process is based on a psychoacoustic model of human hearing and determines what signal-to-noise ratio (SNR) is acceptable for each individual frequency coefficient. The frequency components, after being coarsely quantized to the precision deemed appropriate by the bit allocation process, are multiplexed into the audio elementary bit stream.

In each model, the decoder reverses the process, using the bit allocation information to properly unpack the bit stream and dequantize the samples. The resulting reconstructed frequency coefficients are applied to the synthesis filter bank, which reconstructs the time domain signal. It is understood that this process is not error-free, but the algorithms selected attempt to constrain the artifacts so that they are inaudible.

PERCEPTUAL CODING OF MULTICHANNEL AUDIO

Composite coding techniques can be used to code sound services consisting of more than one channel. These techniques use the information redundancy in the different independent channels so that the bit rate does not increase in proportion to the number of channels.

Composite coding techniques take advantage not only of the correlation in the signal but also in the binaural perception of the signal. A combination of the following effects may be employed:

1. The processing capacity of the human auditory system is limited in its ability to perceive certain details of individual sound channels in a multi-channel environment. A common masking threshold can exploit this interchannel masking.

2. A portion of the multichannel signal set does not contribute to localization of the sound sources. This portion may be reproduced by any speaker. This is termed reduction of sound separation or dynamic cross talk.

3. Certain signals contain interchannel coherent portions which could be transmitted by one channel. This is termed reduction of redundancy.

4. The bit rate required per channel is dependent on the source signal. The dynamic bit rate of the center and individual surround signals may not vary in a completely correlated manner and may even be uncorrelated, resulting in a smoothing effect of the overall bit-rate peaks.

SOUND SERVICES

A packetized data stream supported by packet identification headers and descriptors provides a flexible mechanism for carrying a multitude of sound services. A system which also allows flexibility in the use of audio data compression technology offers the opportunity of encoding a range of services, including multilingual services. By providing a range of compression levels and channel formats, different services can be encoded into bit streams using coding algorithms that are appropriate to the service and do not exceed the data capacity of the channel. This capability leads to the efficient use of the data channel.

The ITU has focused its work on two systems: an MPEG-1 backward-compatible system described in ISO/IEC 13818-3[4] and known as the MPEG-2 system, and a non-backward-compatible system known as AC-3.[5]

Both systems provide for a range of multichannel services from a single channel (monaural) to 5.1 channels for each service. One or more services, each comprised of between 1 and 5.1 channels, can be accommodated depending on the data capacity of the multiplexed bit stream. The notation method used in this chapter describes the number of channels provided by a specific service as F/S, where F represents the number of "front" channels and S represents the number of surround channels. A stereo service is represented by the notation 2/0, whereas the full 5.1 channel service is represented by the notation 3.1/2 or $3^+/2$. A typical speaker placement is shown in Figure 5-5. Both systems provide compression mechanisms that produce bit streams as low as 32 kbits/s for voice/dialogue services to 384 kbits/s for 5.1 channel sound reproduction. Both systems provide for main and associated services. Both systems allow for transmission of one or two independent sound channels, as well as matrixed services which may include L, C, R (Left, Center, Right) and surroundsound. The surroundsound options include a single channel (S) or a surroundsound pair [SL (Surround Left), SR (Surround Right)]. A low-frequency enhancement (LFE) channel capability may be added to any of the matrixed services.

The LFE channel has a limited frequency range (20–120 Hz) and allows the listener to extend the low frequency content of the sound format in terms of both frequency and level. It essentially duplicates the subwoofer channel used in digital film sound formats. The LFE channel may be coded at a lower bit rate and constitutes the ".1" in the "5.1" notation (or the "+" in the "5+" notation).

Both systems are constructed to allow the listener's "appliance" (i.e., television receiver, computer, etc.) to recognize the number of sound channels encoded and decoded and to reproduce the sound service appropriately for the number of speakers provided.

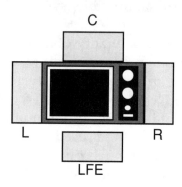

Figure 5-5. Surroundsound.

The AC-3 system provides for eight different service types defined in a 3-bit *bit stream mode* (bsmod) code (see Table 5-1).

The complete main audio service (CM) is the normal mode of operation with all elements of the complete audio program assumed to be present. The CM service may be comprised of any number of channels from 1 to 5.1.

Table 5-1. AC-3 Service Types.[6]

bsmod	Service Type
0	Complete main audio service, complete (CM)
1	Music and effects audio service (ME)
2	Associated service: visually impaired (VI)
3	Associated service: hearing impaired (HI)
4	Associated service: dialog (D)
5	Associated service: commentary (C)
6	Associated service: emergency flash message (E)
7	Associated service: voice-over (VO)

The music and effects audio service (ME) consists of all elements of an audio program except for dialog. The ME service may be comprised of any number of channels from 1 to 5.1. Dialog from one or more associated services must be added to form a complete program. A sporting event broadcast in different languages is a good example of the use of the ME and multiple D services with the event background sound contained in the ME service accompanied by multiple D services, each providing commentary in a different language.

The VI service is a single-channel (1/0) service intended to convey a narrative description of the picture content for use by the visually impaired. The combination of the main program audio and the VI service allows the visually impaired listener to follow the on-screen activity, adding to the understanding of the program. This service is intended to be decoded along with the CM or ME services and mixed into appropriate loudspeaker channels (e.g., typically the C loudspeaker in a 3/* or 1/0 arrangement or into both the L and R loudspeakers as a phantom center in a 2/* arrangement). The choice of the channel could also be left to the listener or the service could be delivered to the VI user as a discrete output such as headphones in order not to disturb other individuals watching the program).

The HI service is a single-channel (1/0) service intended to convey dialog which has been processed for increased intelligibility for use by the hearing impaired. This service is intended to be decoded along with the CM or ME services and mixed into appropriate loudspeaker channels (e.g., typically the C loudspeaker in a 3/* or 1/0 arrangement or into both the L and R loudspeakers as a phantom center in a 2/* arrangement) with the mixing level determined by the hearing-impaired listener. The choice of the channel could also be left to the listener or the service could be delivered to the HI user as a discrete output such as headphones in order not to disturb other individuals watching the program.

The D service provides dialog intended to be mixed into an ME service which, by definition, does not contain dialog. The D service can be either a single-channel (1/0) or a two-channel (2/0) service. This service is intended to be mixed into the appropriate loudspeaker channels. During those instances when dialog is not present, the D service can be removed and the data capacity assigned to another service. The D service provides an efficient method for simultaneously delivering multilanguage services. Multiple D services can be used in conjunction with an ME main audio service. At the receiver, the system demultiplexer will select the appropriate D service indicated by the listener and deliver it to the audio decoder to be mixed with the ME service.

The C service contains a single (1/0) channel of commentary. The commentary service differs from the D service in that the contents are considered an enhancement to the service instead of necessary program content. The decoder mixes the C service with the CM or ME services at the discretion of the listener. When C services are provided, the receiver may notify the listener of C service availability and allow the listener the option of selecting a C service for decoding and mixing. Typical uses seen for C services are additional commentary during sporting events or at different levels of understanding during documentary or educational programming.

The E or emergency flash service is a high-priority service contained in a single (1/0) channel. When this service type appears in the service multiplex, it must be routed to the audio decoder, which decodes and reproduces the service while *muting* the main service. The E service is intended to allow insertion of emergency announcements. Sound services associated with the program do not necessarily have to be replaced in order for the emergency message to get through. The transport demultiplexer gives priority to this type of audio service. The E service is intended to be reproduced as a 1/0 service (e.g., typically the C loudspeaker in a 3/* or 1/0 arrangement or into both the L and R loudspeakers as a phantom center in a 2/* arrangement). The E service could be used in nonemergency applications whenever the broadcaster desires to substitute a higher-priority single-channel message.

The VO or voice-over service is a single-channel (1/0) service. When received, it is decoded along with the CM or ME services and mixed into appropriate loudspeaker channels (e.g., the C loudspeaker in a 3/* or 1/0 arrangement or into both the L and R loudspeakers as a phantom center in a 2/* arrangement). The voice-over service commandeers the dynamic range control function, disabling the listener's control of the dynamic range compression function. This allows the program source to control the main program audio levels in order to allow the voice-over to be heard. The VO service has a priority second only to the E service. The VO service is similar to the E, except that instead of replacing the main audio service when detected by the audio decoder, the decoder mixes the VO channel into the center of the main audio service (e.g., the C loudspeaker in a 3/* or 1/0 arrangement or into both the L and R loudspeakers as a phantom center in a 2/* arrangement). The optional listener control of the main service dynamic range compression is defeated and the reproduction level of both the main audio service and the VO service are under the control of the program service provider. The VO service allows voice-overs to be added to an existing encoded audio elementary bit stream without requiring the audio to be decoded to baseband and reencoded.

Each audio elementary stream may be in any language. Multiple language services can be provided, each as a main audio service in a range of services varying from 1/0 to 3.1/2 and a range of quality from 64 to 384 kbits/s, depending on the number of services that must be accommodated and the data capacity of the multiplexed bit stream. As an example, two language services could be accommodated, each as a 2/0 service at bit rates as low as 128 kbits/s each, for a total of 256 kbits/s.

How MPEG Codes Audio[7,8]

During the years 1988 to 1992, the International Organization for Standardization (ISO) developed a standard on the coding of associated audio for digital storage media. The effort resulted in a standard for coding PCM audio signals at sampling rates of 32, 44.1, and 48 kHz at bit rates in the range 32–192 kbits/s for monaural services and 64–384 kbits/s for stereo audio services. A three-layer concept was developed to support a broad range of recording applications with differing requirements with the levels providing differing amounts of complexity at the encoder and decoder. The three layers are described in ISO Standard 11172-3 and are collectively known as the MPEG-1 audio standard. Layer II of the ISO 11172-3 coding standard is identical with the MUSICAM system.

In all three layers, the PCM input audio signal is converted from the time domain into the frequency domain using a filter bank consisting of 32 subbands. In Layers I and II (see Figure 5-6), the 32 subband representations of the input audio signal stream are quantized and coded under the control of a psychoacoustic model. Layer I is a simplified version for applications where very low data rates are not required. Layer II adds redundancy removal and more precise quantization to further reduce the number of bits required to represent the original sound signal.

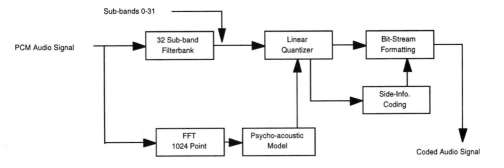

Figure 5-6. MPEG-1 Layers I and II.

In Layer III, additional frequency resolution is provided through the use of a hybrid filter bank that further operates on each of the 32 subbands with a linear transform on 18 subband samples in each subband. Layer III (see Figure 5-7) also utilizes nonuniform quantization, adaptive segmentation, and entropy coding of the quantized values to achieve greater bit-rate reduction.

The ISO/IEC MPEG-2 audio service (ISO/IEC 13818-3) is a backward-compatible multichannel audio channel extension of the MPEG-1 stereo audio service. The MPEG-2 service is capable of providing 5.1 audio channels while ensuring that the existing two-channel decoders will still be able to decode compatible stereo information. The backward compatibility is achieved through the use of compatibility matrices using defined down-mix coefficients. The mechanisms for handling the additional multichannel data that provide backward compatibility are shown in Figures 5-8 and 5-9.

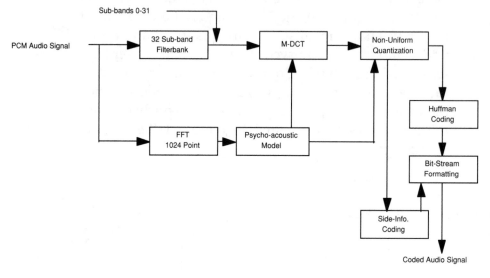

Figure 5-7. MPEG-1 Layer III.

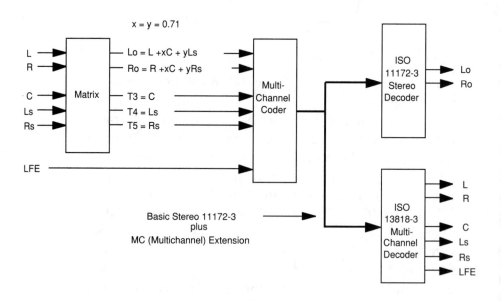

Figure 5-8. MPEG Multichannel Extension.

The variable length of the MPEG-1 Ancillary Data implies that it can be used either to carry the C, LS, RS, and LFE (T3, T4, and T5) information or that it can be used to carry a second stereo program (L2, R2). A multichannel decoder can take full advantage of the data stream, whereas a standard, two-channel MPEG-1 audio decoder ignores the additional data and provides a basic stereo service.

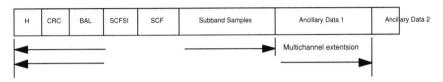

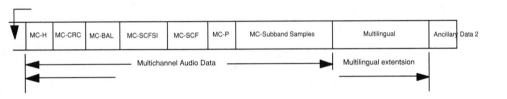

Figure 5-9. MPEG Multichannel Extension Format.

HOW AC-3 CODES AUDIO[9, 10, 11, 12]

The AC-3 system uses a hybrid backward/forward adaptive bit allocation technique (see Figure 5-10). The technique uses a core backward adaptive bit allocation routine which runs in both the encoder and decoder. The core routine is relatively simple and based on a specific psychoacoustic model. The core routine is driven by the spectral envelope and the spectral envelope information is also part of the encoded audio data delivered to the decoder. The spectral envelope and the analysis and synthesis filter banks all have the same time and frequency resolution.

The AC-3 system uses a forward adaptive core routine to enable psychoacoustic model parameter adjustment and bit allocation. The core bit allocation routine makes assumptions about the masking properties of the signal construct and the human hearing system. Certain para-meters of the model are explicitly transmitted within the bit stream. The encoder, however, can perform bit allo-cation based on psychoacoustic models of any complex-ity and compare the result to the bit allocation based on the core routine. If a better match can be made to a more ideal allocation by altering one or more of the parame-ters used by the core routine, the encoder can make the adjustment and inform the decoder of the change by transmitting the new parameter values. In the case where it is not possible to approach an ideal allocation by means of parameter changes, the encoder can explic-itly send allocation information. The AC-3 syntax allows the encoder to send bit allocation information, which allows the bit allocation in small frequency regions to be increased or decreased. The final bit allocation used by the encoder and the decoder must be identical and con-sists of the preset decoder core routine modified by the parameter changes and bit allocation information pro-vided by the encoder.

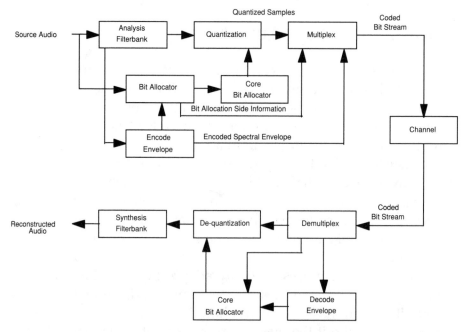

Figure 5-10. Hybrid Bit Allocation System.

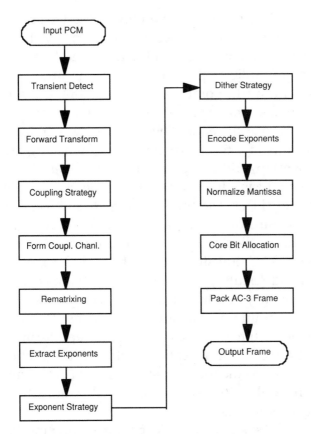

Figure 5-11. AC-3 Process.

The AC-3 process (see Figure 5-11) uses an oddly stacked time-domain aliasing cancellation (TDAC) filter bank. Overlapping blocks of 512 windowed samples are transformed into 256 frequency domain points. Audio, sampled at 48 kHz, is formed into blocks that are 10.66 ms in length, with transforms performed every 5.33 ms. A group of six blocks are coded into a single AC-3 frame. The blocks of 512 samples are formed from 256 new samples and 256 samples from the previous blocks. The overlapping of blocks assists in preventing audible blocking artifacts. During some transient signal conditions, the length of the transform is reduced by 50% in order to improve time resolution at the expense of frequency resolution.

A proprietary 512-point window is used to achieve the best trade-off between close-in frequency selectivity and faraway rejection. The windowing operation involves vector multiplication of the 512-point audio sample block with a 512-point window function. The window function has a value of 1.0 at the center and tapers down to near-zero at the ends. The shape of the window function results in a reconstruction free of blocking artifacts after overlap/add processing at the decoder.

The analysis filter bank is based on the fast Fourier transform (FFT). The time-domain aliasing cancellation (TDAC) transform used allows the redundancy introduced in the blocking process to be removed. The input to the TDAC transform consists of 512 time-domain points and results in 256 frequency domain coefficients. The frequency resolution of the filter bank is 93.75 Hz with minimum time resolution of 2.67 ms. The full resolution of the filter bank is employed except during a portion of the core bit allocation routine. Bit allocation can occur down to the individual transform coefficient level with the ability to assign different allocations to neighboring coefficients.

The AC-3 system uses an exponent coding mechanism to reduce the amount of data necessary. First, the raw exponents of the six blocks included in a single AC-3 frame are examined for block-to-block differences. If the differences are small, a single exponent set is generated which is usable by all six blocks. If the exponents show significant differences within a frame, then exponent sets are formed over blocks where the changes are not significant. Exponents for adjacent frequencies rarely differ by more than ±2 (1 represents a 6-dB-level change) due to the nature of the frequency response of the individual filters in the analysis filter bank. Exponents are encoded differentially in frequency to take advantage of this fact. The first exponent in the block, considered the zero-frequency, DC term, is set at its absolute value and the rest of the exponents as the difference between the current exponent and the prior exponent. The values are limited to the set +2, +1, 0, –1, and –2.

Three different encoding mechanisms are employed depending on the audio content. When fine frequency resolution is required for relatively steady signals and the spectral envelope remains relatively constant over many blocks, three differentials are encoded into a 7-bit word. This encodes each exponent into 2.33 bits and is termed D15 coding. When the spectrum is not stable, it is beneficial to send the spectral estimate more often. In order to keep the data overhead from becoming excessive, two additional modes (medium and low) of frequency resolution are used. The medium resolution mode, termed D25, transmits information for every other frequency coefficient, resulting in a data rate of 2.33 bits per exponent pair or 1.16 bits per exponent. This mode is typically used when the spectrum is relatively stable over two to three audio blocks and then changes significantly. Use of the D25 mode does not allow the spectral envelope to accurately follow all of the troughs in a very tonal spectrum but does follow the peaks. The final mode, termed D45, is transmitted for every four coefficients, halving again the data rate, and is typically used during transients in single audio blocks. Transient signals do not typically require fine frequency resolution because by their nature they are wide-band signals. The result is a transmitted spectral envelope with fine frequency resolution for relatively steady-state signals and fine time resolution for transient signals. The final coding efficiency for exponents, including the gain due to sharing across multiple blocks, is typically 0.39 bits per exponent. Each coded audio block contains a 2-bit *exponent strategy* field, allowing for four strategies: D15, D25, D45, or REUSE. For most signal conditions, a D15-coded exponent set is sent during the first audio block in the frame and the following audio blocks reuse the same exponent set. During transient conditions, exponents are sent more often. The encoder exponent strategy may be improved over time (made extensible) and because it is explicitly encoded into the data stream, all decoders will respond to the new strategy.

The precision of the mantissas is dependent on the precision of the word length of the input audio source. Typically this precision is on the order of 16–20 bits but may be as high as 24 bits. The AC-3 system quantizes the normalized mantissa to a precision of between 0 and 16 bits. The number of bits allocated to each mantissa is determined by the core bit allocation routine, which is identical in both the encoder and decoder. The AC-3 core bit allocation routine is considered backward adaptive in that the encoded audio information represented by the spectral envelope is fed back into the encoder and is used to compute the final bit allocation. The spectral envelope represents the power spectral density (PSD) of the signal. There may be as many as 252 PSD values sent, depending on the number of exponents required and the desired audio bandwidth and sampling rate. In addition to the power spectral density, the bit allocation routine is also driven by the convolution of a spreading function matching the human hearing masking curve. The computational load is reduced by converting the PSD array into smaller banded PSD arrays. At low frequencies, the band size is 1. At high frequencies, the band size is 16. The bands increase in size proportional to the widening of the human ear's critical bands, and the masking curve indicates the level of quantizing that can be tolerated as a function of frequency. The masking curve is subtracted from the signal spectrum in the log domain, yielding the required signal-to-noise ratio (SNR) as a function of frequency. The SNR values are mapped into a set of bit allocation pointers which indicate the quantization appropriate to each transform coefficient mantissa. The encoder counts the number of bits to determine if the bit allocation has used up the available number of bits. (All available bits are contained in a common bit pool which is available to all channels.) When more bits are available, the individual mantissa SNRs may be increased until all bits are used. If too many bits have been allocated, the individual mantissa SNRs may be decreased and/or a technique termed *coupling* may be applied.

Within narrow frequency bands, the human ear detects high-frequency (above 2 kHz) localization based on the signal envelope rather than the detailed signal waveform. Direction is determined by the interaural time delay of the signal envelope. The ear is not able to detect the direction of two high-frequency signals which are closely spaced in frequency. Coupling takes advantage of this phenomenon by combining the high-frequency content of individual channels and sending the individual channel signal envelopes along the combined coupling channel. The frequency at which coupling begins is the *coupling frequency*. Care must be taken so that the phase of the signals to be combined does not result in cancellation. The encoder measures the signal power of the input channels in narrow frequency bands, as well as the power in the same bands in the coupled channel. The encoder generates *coupling coordinates* for each individual channel, which indicate the ratio of the original signal power to the coupling channel power within a band. The coupling channel is encoded in the same manner as the individual channels, resulting in a spectral envelope and a set of quantized mantissas. Data in the channels included in the coupling are sent but only up to the coupling frequency. Above that point, only the coupling coordinates are transmitted. The individual channel coupling coordinates are multiplied by the channel coupling coefficients in the decoder to produce the high-frequency coefficients of the coupled channels. Coupling coordinates are encoded with an accuracy of < 0.25 dB. Coupling should be considered a lossy process because some of the detailed information is lost. When employed, coupling coordinates are sent in block 0 of each frame. The coupling coordinates need not be sent every block if the signal envelope is steady but can be reused by the decoder. The encoder determines when new coupling coordinates need to be sent.

The AC-3 syntax forms a 16-bit sync word and an 8-bit word which indicates sampling rate and frame size (SI), *bit stream info* (BSI), the 6 transform coded audio blocks (32 ms of audio), and a 16-bit CRC error-check code into an AC-3 sync frame. The BSI contains information about the number of channels coded, dialog level, language code, and information on associated services. A 5-bit field in the BSI indicates the level of average spoken dialog within the encoded audio program relative to the level of a full-scale 1-kHz sine wave.

The system is designed so that boundaries of sync frames are appropriate for splicing of audio elementary bit streams. When bit stream splices occur randomly, frames which are incomplete will not pass the decoder's error detection test, causing the decoder to mute. The decoder then enters a sync search mode. Once the sync code is found and synchronization is achieved, audio service begins again. The outage will be on the order of two frames or about 64 ms.

AC-3 syntax includes a *dynamic range control word* which may be encoded into each audio block, allowing alteration of the reproduced audio. The control has a range of ±24 dB. Some broadcasters highly compress the dynamic range of the audio and fully modulate the audio channel. Sometimes the entertainment portion of the program will have a more natural dynamic range with some headroom, but the commercial messages may not. This results in significant level differences between program segments and between broadcast services. The dynamic range control word can be used in the receiver to reduce the amount of dynamic range compression introduced, allowing the listeners to control the dynamic range of the programs.[13]

END NOTES

1. Audio Engineering Society, AES3-1992/ANSI S4.40-1992, "AES Recommended Practice for Digital Audio Engineering," serial transmission format for two-channel linearly represented digital audio data.

2. The six channels are Left (L), Center (C), Right (R), Left Surround (LS), Right Surround (RS), and a "sub-woofer" low-frequency enhancement channel (LFE). The limited capacity of the LFE channel has led to its being described as the ".1" channel, with the full service noted as consisting of 5.1 channels.

3. The term *compression* as used in this context means the compression or reduction of the amount of digital data used to represent the audio signal and not compression of the dynamic range of the audio signal.

4. ISO/IEC 13818-3, Draft International Standard, "Information Technology—Generic Coding of Moving Pictures and Associated Audio: Audio," 10 May 1994.

5. United States Advanced Television System Committee, ATSC Draft Standard, "Digital Audio Compression," Document T3/251, 25 July 1994.

6. ATSC Draft Standard, "Digital Audio Compression (AC-3)," ATSC Document T3/251, 25 July 1994, p. 18.

7. ISO/IEC 11172-3, International Standard, "Coding of Moving Pictures and Associated Audio for Digital Storage Media up to About 1.5 Mbits/s—Audio Part," November 1992.

8. ISO/IEC 13818-3, Draft International Standard, "Information Technology—Generic Coding of Moving Pictures and Associated Audio: Audio," 10 May 1994.

9. ATSC Draft Standard, "Digital Audio Compression," ATSC Document T3/251, 25 July 1994.

10. ATSC, "Guide to the Use of the ATSC Digital Television Standard," Chapter 6, *Audio Systems*, ATSC Document T3/259, 31 August 1994.

11. ATSC Draft Standard, "ATSC Digital Television Standard," Annex II, ATSC Document T3/258, 31 August 1994.

12. C.C. Todd, G.A. Davidson, et al., "AC-3: Flexible perceptual coding for audio transmission and storage," Audio Engineering Society Convention, Amsterdam, 26 February 1994 (submitted).

13. ITU Document 11-3/67, "Tutorial on Digital Terrestrial Television Broadcasting in the VHF/UHF Bands," 15 December 1994.

6

Modulation: The Physical Transport

Digital modulation is an outgrowth of the more familiar methods of analog modulation such as amplitude, frequency, and phase modulation. The modulation techniques being used in systems proposed or under development for digital terrestrial television broadcasting (DTTB) services fall into two categories: single- or dual-carrier systems or multicarrier systems. Both approaches must deal with the primary channel impairments due to multipath reception, co-channel interference from existing analog television services, adjacent channel interference from existing analog television services, and impulse interference. The goal of a DTTB service is to accommodate a data rate sufficient to allow either a single-channel high-definition television (HDTV) service or multiple-program standard television services.

INTRODUCTION

Work reported by ITU-R Task Group 11/3 shows that a digital terrestrial television broadcasting (DTTB) service can provide compressed high-definition television (HDTV) program services at a bit rate of approximately

20 Mbits/s.[1,2] Accommodating a data rate of approximately 20 Mbits/s requires that the modulation scheme provide for 4 bits/s/Hz in a 6-MHz bandwidth channel and 3 Mbits/s/Hz in a 7- or 8-MHz bandwidth channel.

Data rates of up to 4 bits/s/Hz can be achieved by using either a 16 QAM (quadrature-amplitude modulation), 4 VSB (vestigial sideband), or 16 PSK (phase shift keying) modulation mechanism. All three mechanisms may be used to modulate either a single carrier with a high data rate signal or to modulate multiple carriers, dividing the total data rate among the carriers as appropriate. The error characteristics of practical terrestrial transmission channels require, however, that error correction coding be included. Using some portion of the total bit capacity to provide error correction and protection coding tends to reduce the effective data payload in practical systems. The modulator subsystem, therefore, consists of two parts. The first part takes the input transport data stream and applies processes to code the data for use in the transmission channel that will make the data more robust. These channel coding processes include data interleaving and other error protection and correction coding mechanisms, taking into consideration broadcast coverage area desired, interference characteristics of the channel, and other planning factors. The second part involves conversion of the resulting coded data stream into an analog representation to be applied to the transmitter.

GENERIC BLOCK DIAGRAM

A block diagram of a generic modulator subsystem is shown in Figure 6-1. The blocks that appear prior to the **Mapper** constitute the first part of the subsystem, the channel coding segment designed to prepare the data stream for transmission, whereas the mapper and the blocks that follow constitute the mechanism use to create a modulated carrier that transmits the data stream over the air.

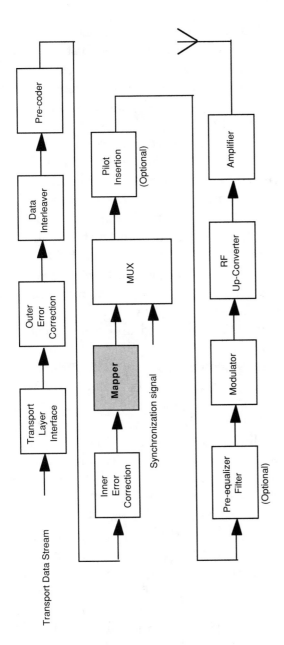

Figure 6-1. Modulator Block Diagram.

The **Transport Layer Interface** prepares the incoming data stream for presentation to the **Outer Error Correction** coder. Most error protection schemes use two stages of coding termed an outer error-correction code and an inner error-correction code, supplemented by interleaving/scrambling processes. The first stage, shown as the Outer Error Correction in Figure 6-1, is generally based on a coding mechanism known as Reed–Solomon forward error correction (RS-FEC) coding. This coding mechanism adds extra, redundant bits to each packet or block of data in a scheme similar to that of a complex parity error-correction mechanism, allowing detection and correction of individual bit errors in the block of data. The Reed–Solomon code used needs to be able to accommodate a total protected information packet equal to or greater than the MPEG-2 transport packet of 188 bytes (1504 bits) and an error-correcting capability of "T." The system requirements can be accommodated by a Reed–Solomon code of (255, 255-2T, T), where the protected information part equals 255-2T. Burst errors of up to T bytes (8 x T bits in length) at the input of the RS decoder can be corrected successfully.

One possible solution adds 20 Reed–Solomon parity bytes to this data packet for error correction, bringing the total to 208 bytes or 1664 bits to be transmitted per data segment. In this example, T equals 10 bytes or 80 bits. This means that the data payload represents a maximum of 188/208 (90.38%) of the total system capacity. The vestigial sideband (VSB) system proposed for North America provides data synchronization within a transmitted frame of data and, within the modulator, drops the MPEG-2 sync byte from the data packet. The data block size is, therefore, 187 bytes and the RS (207, 188, 10) coding of this packet produces a payload efficiency of 207/187 or 90.33%.[3] The Scandinavian HD-DIVINE system employs the RS (204, 188, 8) code used in the DVB specifications for an efficiency of 92.16%.[4]

The Outer Error Correction stage can be followed by a **data interleaver** which may include a data randomizer. The data randomizer can consist of a pseudo-random binary generator, the output of which is exclusive-ORd with the input data. The application of a data randomizer on the input data streams is intended to ensure that the resulting data content distribution is Gaussian in nature. The only parts of the data stream not randomized are those bytes that provide the synchronization function.[5] An example of a randomizer generator polynomial is

$$G_{16} = X^{16} + X^{13} + X^{12} + X^{11} + X^7 + X^6 + X^3 + X + 1$$

The 16-bit pseudo-random binary sequence is initialized with a known value [e.g., F180(h)] at the beginning of the data field.

The data interleaver is a mechanism employed to reorganize the data stream so that it is less vulnerable to bursts of errors. In the example shown in Figure 6-2, interleaving is provided to a depth of about one-sixth of the data field using a 52-data intersegment convolutional byte interleaver. Bytes are kept whole so that the Trellis encoder process, applied immediately after, processes consecutive symbols from the same byte.

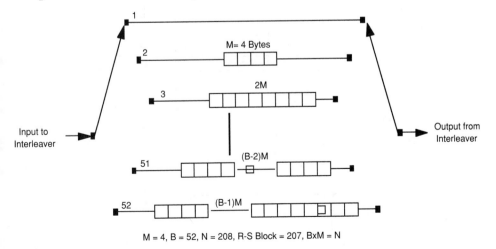

M = 4, B = 52, N = 208, R-S Block = 207, BxM = N

Figure 6-2. Data Interleaver.

The coded data stream may be applied to a **Precoder** prior to the inner error-correction coder. The precoder organizes the data packets into frames of data. In the example shown in Figure 6-3, each data frame consists of two data fields with each data field consisting of 313 data segments. The first data segment of each data field is the **Data Field Sync** segment, a unique synchronizing signal which includes a training signal for potential use by an equalizer in the receiver. The remaining 312 data segments contain the data from one 188-byte transport packet as modified by the Reed–Solomon encoder process. Since the data stream has also passed through the interleaver, the data in a data segment comes from several transport data stream packets. In a multicarrier COFDM system, the outer interleaver interleaves the information between different COFDM symbols and, therefore, can be regarded as a time interleaver.[6]

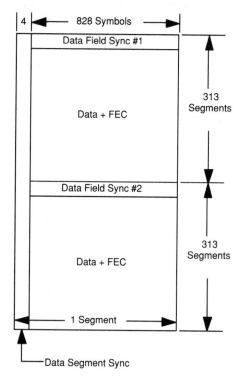

Figure 6-3. Data Frame.

The data interleaver can be followed by a second stage of error coding, shown as the **Inner Error Correction** block in Figure 6-1. The inner error correction may be implemented as a Trellis encoder mechanism and is based on convolutional coding. A simple convolutional coder (see Figure 6-4) replaces each bit applied to the input with two bits. The content of the two bits is dependent on both the state of the input bit and the internal state of the coder. Not all sequences of bits are allowed, and errors introduced in the received sequence will cause unacceptable transition paths in the received sequence in the decoder. Allowable transition paths are shown in Figure 6-5. The errors can be corrected by finding the nearest acceptable path.[7]

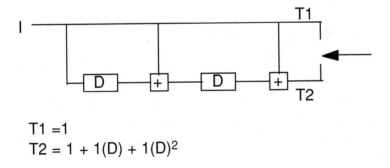

$$T1 = 1$$
$$T2 = 1 + 1(D) + 1(D)^2$$

Figure 6-4. Simple Convolutional Coder.

In the example of the VSB system proposed for North America, the second stage of error protection consists of a 2/3 rate Trellis code. The 2/3 rate (R = 2/3) Trellis code encodes one bit of a two-bit pair into two output bits using a 1/2 convolutional code, whereas the other input bit is retained as pre-coded. 2/3 rate Trellis coding requires a total of 3/2 times the number of bits per RS-FEC packet or (3/2) x 1656 bits = 2496 bits per packet. This means that in the specific proposed VSB system, the data payload now represents a maximum of (2/3) x (187/207) (60.22%) of the total system capacity. This sample implementation uses a Trellis coding mechanism with 12 identical Trellis coders to operate on the interleaved data. The Trellis code interleaver encodes symbols (0, 12, 24, 36, 48...) as one group, symbols (1, 13, 25, 37, 49...) as the second group, and so forth until all 12 groups are accommodated.

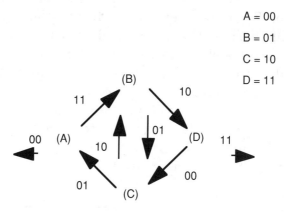

Figure 6-5. Transition Path Diagram.

In the COFDM system, the inner interleaver interleaves the data across the carriers and, therefore, can be regarded as providing frequency interleaving. The interleaving pattern is generated by a random generator. In a multipath fading condition, there exists an optimum interleaving pattern for a given fading condition. In a wireless environment, it is not possible to chose a good interleaving pattern that is good for all receivers at the same time, since they will experience different fading patterns depending upon local receiving conditions. The solution is to use a time-varying interleaving pattern.

This will ensure that any one receiver will, irrespective of the fading pattern, receive both "good" and "bad" interleaving patterns. This will give a performance when combined with the outer interleaving that, to the greatest possible extent, avoids interruptions in service in a multipath fading condition.

In the specific implementation used in the COFDM-6 system, the inner error correction code uses Trellis Coded Modulation (TCM), which combines coding and modulation in one step to achieve high coding gains without affecting the bandwidth of the signal. In the TCM encoder, each symbol of n bits is mapped into a constellation of n + 1 bits using a set-partitioning rule.[8] TCM coding only increases the constellation size and uses the additional redundancy to Trellis code the signal. The 64 QAM modulation scheme takes significant advantage of the Trellis coding and the proper implementation of this function, which includes decoding with the Viterbi algorithm[9] and provides optimum channel recovery and correction of the original data stream. QAM mapping is really a vector mapping. A digital system has the advantage of combining multiple steps into a single step through the use of look-up tables. The I and Q information present in each frame may be used as an input address to a look-up table. The result of this mathematically complex addressing is a signal expressed in the digital form as a data stream but representing amplitude and phase information of the coded frame.

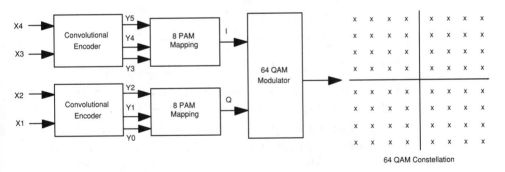

Figure 6-6. 64-QAM Trellis Coding.

In the COFDM-6 system, therefore, the TCM code consists of two uni-dimensional rate 2/3 TCM codes (see Figure 6-6), which result in a 64 QAM constellation. A Trellis interleaver is also implemented following the TCM encoder to decorrelate short bursts of transmission errors. The inner code interleaver interleaves the information between the different carriers and is, therefore, a frequency interleaver. The task of the inner interleaver is to avoid long error bursts into the Viterbi decoder, as this will produce long error bursts at the output as well. At high bit error rates, error bursts will occur at the Viterbi decoder, but the outer interleaving distributes these error bursts onto several Reed–Solomon code words.[10]

8-Level Symbol Mapping

Z2, Z1, Z0	R
000	−7
001	−5
010	−3
011	−1
100	+1
101	+3
110	+5
111	+7

Figure 6-7. Simple (D/A) Bit Mapper.

The output of the Trellis coder is fed to the mapper, which converts the data stream into **symbols**. As a simple example, each data segment could consist of 832 symbols with the first four symbols used to represent the sync byte of the 188-byte transport packet and the remaining 828 symbols used to transport the 187 data bytes of the transport packet, including the error protection overhead bits. The sync byte (first four symbols) could be transmitted as binary levels, whereas the remaining 828 symbols could be transmitted carrying three bits per symbol. Therefore, the 828 data symbols are mapped into 1 of 8 ($2^3 = 8$) levels (−7 to +7) as shown in Figure 6-7. Because the sync byte symbols are transmitted at binary levels, these symbols are approximately 12 dB more resistant to noise than the other symbols being sent at eight different levels.

The output of the mapper is fed to a multiplexer (MUX) where the four-symbol data segment sync binary signal is added, as shown in Figure 6-8 along with the data field synchronization signal.

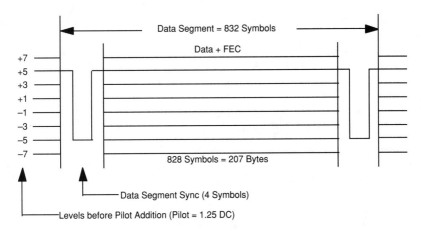

Figure 6-8. Data Segment Sync.

As noted earlier, each data field begins with a *data field sync* segment, as shown in Figure 6-9. The data field sync consists of binary (0, 1) pseudo-random sequences of 511 and 63 symbols followed by 12 symbols at the end that are a repeat from the previous active data segment. The three 63-bit sequences in the data field sync alternate polarity from one field to the next, and as there are two data field syncs within a single data frame, the average value of the data field sync is held close to zero. This implies that if a DC pilot is added prior to transmission, the desired value of the pilot is not altered. (The 511-bit sequence is not inverted from field to field.)

The binary pseudo-random sequences of 511 (PS-511) and 63 (PS-63) are, in this example, generated by shift registers of length 9 and 6, respectively. (PS-511) = X^9 + $X^7 + X^6 + X^4 + X^3 + X + 1$, with an initialization state = (0 1000 0000). (PS-63) = $X^6 + X + 1$, with an initialization state = (10 0000). The data segment and data field sync are inserted in the MUX after the Reed–Solomon and Trellis coders and are also not interleaved.

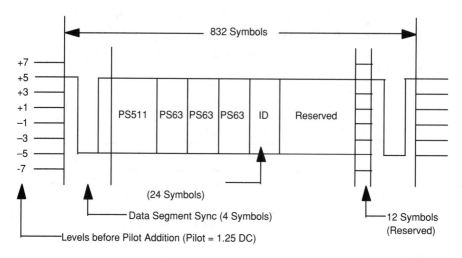

Figure 6-9. Data Field Sync.

MODULATION TECHNIQUES

The modulation techniques proposed for consideration by TG11/3 for either single- or multiple-carrier systems include vestigial sideband modulation (VSB) and quadrature amplitude modulation (QAM).

VSB is a compromise between double-sideband amplitude modulation (AM) and single-sideband AM. It includes a small part of the lower sideband with the full upper sideband. Sloped filtering at the transmitter and/or at the receiver attenuates the lower end of the band to compensate for the duplication of the low-frequency sidebands. The system proposed for North America uses a combination of 8-VSB for the majority of the data stream symbols and 2-VSB for the synchronization portion of the data stream. The 8-VSB coding maps three bits into one of eight signal levels ranging from –7 to +7 as noted above. The 2-VSB coding is binary coded into one of two levels. The system uses a symbol rate[11] of 10.76 Msymbols/s capable of supporting a data stream payload of 19.349 Mbits/s.[12] The sample system mapper described in the prior section is based on the VSB approach.

QAM technology has been implemented at several levels including 16-QAM, 32-QAM, and 64-QAM. 16-QAM is a digital form of quadrature amplitude modulation that transmits four bits per symbol (4 bits/Hz). The approximately 20-Mbits/s data stream is first converted into 4-bit words. The "16" refers to the fact that 4-bit words can produce 16 ($2^4 = 16$) different possible symbol positions. The symbol rate is clearly one-quarter of the original bit rate, or about 5 Msymbols/s. In a QAM-based system, the mapper shown in the Figure 6-1 block diagram takes a form as shown in Figure 6-10. In a QAM mapper, a simple D-to-A (digital-to-analog) converter converts one pair of bits from the symbol to a four-level signal that is applied to a balanced modulator along with an RF (or IF) carrier to the other input. The other pair of symbol bits is similarly converted into a four-level signal, and is applied to a second balanced modulator operating in quadrature from the first (with the carrier shifted 90°). The two balanced-modulator outputs are combined to produce the 16-QAM signal, centered at the carrier (or intermediate frequency). This output signal can then be heterodyned to the actual transmitted frequency. The constellation produced by the balanced modulator is shown in Figure 6-11. The 32-QAM and 64-QAM are variations on the 16-QAM form of quadrature amplitude modulation that transmit 5 bits per symbol (5 bits/Hz) and 6 bits per symbol (6 bits/Hz), respectively.

At the receiver, there is also a pair of balanced modulators, driven by a local oscillator (LO) shifted by 90° between modulators. The LO must be phase-locked to the original carrier at the transmitter. In the receiver, the carrier phase is recovered from the data by a complex process using phase-locked loops and will not be discussed here. The outputs of the balanced modulators are not ideal square waves but the four-level signals approach square waves that have been filtered to meet the channel bandwidth limitations. In the 16-QAM receiver, the in-phase signal and the quadrature signal are each converted back to 2-bit digital form by a pair of A-to-D (analog-to-digital) converters. The resulting two pairs of bits are then multiplexed to yield a replica of the original 20-Mbits/s data stream.

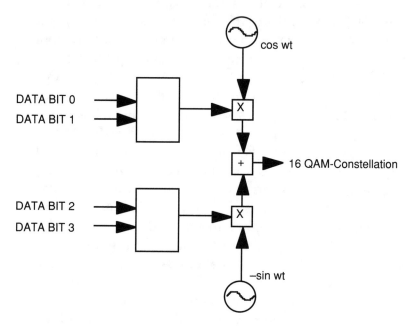

Figure 6-10. 16-QAM Generator.

Among the systems tested were the following: 32-QAM systems delivering rates of 24.39 Mbits/s and 26.43 Mbits/s in a 6-MHz channel; 16-QAM systems at rates of 19.51 Mbits/s and 21.15 Mbits/s in a 6-MHz channel; a dual-carrier 32-QAM system for a total data rate of 24 Mbits/s (the system used one high-priority carrier providing 4.8 Mbits/s service and one low-priority carrier providing 19.2 Mbits/s service in a 6-MHz channel[13]; and a 64-QAM system delivering 34.01 Mbits/s in an 8-MHz channel.[14]

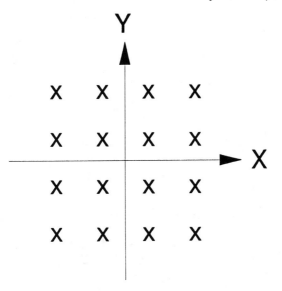

Figure 6-11. 16-QAM Constellation.

SINGLE-CARRIER SYSTEMS

A single-carrier system has been developed using the vestigial side band (VSB) technique in a 6-MHz channel. The VSB modulator accepts a 10.76-MHz 8-VSB coded data signal with the synchronization signals added. This system employs a DC-pilot carrier to allow better signal acquisition under noisy conditions. The DC pilot is created by adding a value of 1.25 to the nominal, mapped signal levels (–7, –5, –3, –1, +1, +3, +5, +7). The channel response is nominally flat across the band except for the transition regions as shown in Figure 6-12. The selectivity of the transition regions is not the same, in order to best accommodate the nature of the vestigial sideband signal. The baseband signals can be converted to analog form and modulated on quadrature intermediate frequency (IF) carriers to create the vestigial sideband IF signal by sideband cancellation. One possible approach would have the IF carrier and the DC pilot = to 44 MHz plus one-quarter of the symbol rate.

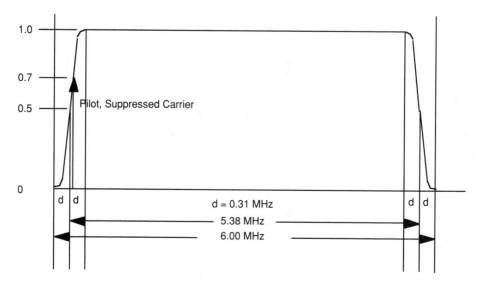

Figure 6-12. VSB in 6-MHz Channel.

MULTICARRIER SYSTEMS

Multicarrier systems spread the data to be transmitted over a large number of independent carriers, each being modulated at a low bit rate and, therefore, a low symbol rate. Effects of the channel frequency selectivity are thus reduced by spreading out fading or impulse noise over many symbols. Orthogonal Frequency Division Multiplexing (OFDM) is a form of multicarrier modulation where the carrier spacing is selected so that each subcarrier within the channel is orthogonal to the other subcarriers, as shown in Figure 6-13. The orthogonal relationship is one which mathematically ensures that during the sampling time for one carrier, all other carriers are at a zero point. The spacing between the carriers is a function of carrier offset and phase stability to protect against intercarrier interference.

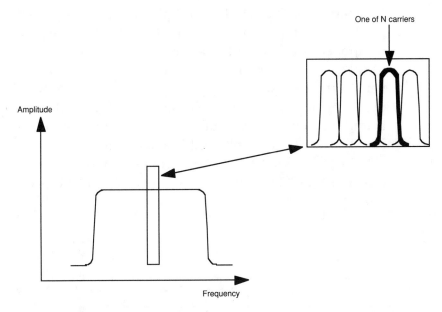

Figure 6-13. OFDM Multiple Carriers.

In order to cope with problems of multipath propagation, a guard interval is added before the beginning of each useful symbol to avoid intersymbol interference. The introduction of a guard interval prior to the beginning of each symbol time protects against multipath distortion where the multipath delay is less than the guard interval. The multipath echoes that are received within the guard interval do not cause intersymbol interference. Resistance to multipath distortion allows consideration of Coded OFDM (COFDM) techniques in single-frequency networks. This gives an additional benefit when compared with traditional modulation techniques such as single-carrier QAM.[15]

In a COFDM system, the modulator in the block diagram shown in Figure 6-1 takes the form shown in Figure 6-14. In the COFDM process incoming data is mapped (MAP) into a number (N) of signal vectors corresponding to the number of carriers used. An Inverse Fast Fourier Transform (IFFT) is performed on the resulting N complex numbers, yielding another set of complex numbers (N'). The set of N' complex numbers is passed through digital-to-analog converters (D/A). The real component (Re) is multiplied by cos wt and the imaginary component (Im) is multiplied by −sin wt to up-convert to the desired carrier. The resulting multiplication products are summed to yield the channel OFDM spectrum. The demodulation process is performed by direct Fast Fourier Transforms. Multicarrier systems based on OFDM technology have been proposed and/or prototyped using QPSK, 4PSK, 8PSK, 16-QAM, and 64-QAM modulation.

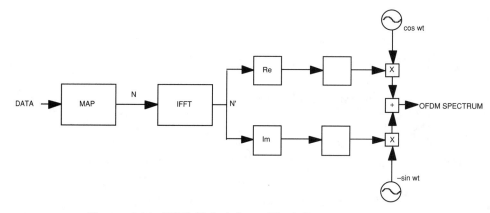

Figure 6-14. OFDM Modulator Block Diagram.

It has been found that the performance of uncoded OFDM with respect to frequency-selective fading under conditions of strong multipath interference is not significantly different from that of an uncoded single-carrier system. COFDM using convolutional coding and interleaving and a concatenated two-code system employing Reed–Solomon techniques showed significant resistance to fading when compared with the uncoded OFDM as shown in Table 6-1.[16] Similarly, uncoded OFDM is particularly sensitive to co-channel or adjacent-channel interference because of the low power in each carrier. In one example, a narrowband interferer could cause a BER of 0.5 on a few carriers of a 1000-carrier OFDM system, leading to a system BER of approximately 10^{-3} at a power 20 dB below that needed to cause a similar BER in a single-carrier system. A COFDM system protected with a rate 0.5, K = 7 convolutional code with 64 out of 512 carriers disabled showed a performance degradation of less than 3 dB. In the case of low-power interference, the OFDM process spreads the energy over a whole symbol period and over many symbols. In the case of high-power impulse interference, the interference can be serious for one symbol period across all the carriers, producing a significant number of errors. However, interleaving and error correction processes of COFDM reduce this problem.[17]

Table 6-1. Protection Ratios into OFDM (dB).

Method	Co-channel	Multiplath (0.5 us)	Noise
QPSK—No Coding	– 3	4	12.5
QPSK—RAte 0.5	– 12	0	7.5
16-QAM—No Coding	5	4.5	21
16-QAM—Rate 0.5	– 6	0	14.5
16-QAM—Rate 0.75	0	0	16.5

END NOTES

1. ATSC Document T3/259, "United States Advanced Television Systems Committee, Guide to the Use of the ATSC Digital Television Standard," 31 August 1994.

2. ITU-R Document 11-3/TEMP/17, 24 October 1994.

3. ATSC Document T3/258, "United States Advanced Television Systems Committee, ATSC Digital Television Standard," 31 August 1994, Annex IV.

4. ITU-R Document 11-3/50, "A Flexible COFDM Modem for the HD-Divine Digital Terrestrial Broadcasting System," 12 October 1994.

5. Unless otherwise noted, the examples used in this chapter are based on the proposed United States Advanced Television Service system as described in ATSC Document T3/258, "United States Advanced Television Systems Committee, ATSC Digital Television Standard," 31 August 1994, Annex IV.

6. "COFDM-6 System Technical Description," 11 July 1995, p. 16.

7. Y. Ninomiya, "Error Management in Digital Terrestrial Television Broadcasting," *ITU/SMPTE Tutorial on Digital Terrestrial Television Broadcasting*, Society of Motion Pictures and Television Engineers, SMPTE, 1994, pp. 107–128.

8. G. Ungerbroeck, "Trellis Coded Modulation with Redundant Signal Set," *IEEE Communications Magazine*, Vol. 27, pp. 5–21, February 1987.

9. J.G. Proakis, *Digital Communications*, McGraw-Hill, 1983.

10. "COFDM-6 System Technical Description," 11 July 1995, p. 16.

11. The symbol rate (Sr) was chosen = 4.5 MHz x (684/286) = 10.762 238 Msymbols/s.

12. In this example, the data capacity of the system (D) is equal to Sr x (828/832) x N x (187/207) x (2/3), where

> Sr is the symbol rate, 828/832 is the data/total symbols ratio, N is the number of bits per symbol = 3, 187/207 is the Reed–Solomon coding overhead factor, and 2/3 is the Trellis coding overhead factor.

Therefore,

$$D = 10.7362 \text{ MHz} \times (828/832) \times (3)(187/207)(2/3)$$
$$= 19.349 \text{ Mbits/s.}$$

13. ITU-R Document 11-3/103, "Progress in HDTV Broadcasting Standards in the United States," 11 October 1993.

14. ITU-R Document 11-3/79, "OFDM Performance and Test Results," 4 October 1993.

15. ITU-R Document 11-3/UK2, "The Use of OFDM for Terrestrial Broadcasting of Digital Television," 3 October 1994.

16. ITU-R Document 11-3/UK3, "Updated Radio Frequency Protection Ratios for OFDM Digital Terrestrial Television," 3 October 1994.

17. ITU-R Document 11-3/UK2, "The Use of OFDM for Terrestrial Broadcasting of Digital Television," 3 October 1994.

7

High-Definition Television

In 1972, the ITU began a study on a new high-definition television (HDTV) service. The goals for this high-definition service included viewing at approximately three times picture height, such that the system would provide images that are virtually transparent to the quality of portrayal perceived in the original scene by a discerning viewer with normal visual acuity. This implied the development of a system with improved motion portrayal, perception of depth, and colorimetry with respect to the current 525- and 625-line television broadcast standards. Such a system would allow viewing on large, wider aspect ratio displays that would leave the viewers with the perception that they were surrounded by the images. The system was also seen as providing a common tool for use in electronic film production and special effects for the cinema, printing, computer imaging, television photography, and a vast array of applications in education, medicine, video conferencing, scientific work, and so forth.

The system was based on the use of new technologies with a heavy dependence on the application of digital technology and has had a radical impact on all aspects of the television chain from program-generation facilities through program distribution and the television receiver itself. A *new era in television broadcasting was brought about by developments in digital television originally conceived to meet the challenges of implementing HDTV service.*

INTRODUCTION

Efforts to achieve international standards for high-definition television (HDTV) were greatly influenced by the various implementation scenarios adopted in different regions of the world. In the area of broadcasting, some countries envisaged the use of direct broadcast satellites as the primary delivery medium, whereas others envisaged terrestrial broadcasting and cable distribution schemes.

The CCIR, the International Radio Consultative Committee, as the section of the International Telecommunications Union (ITU) concerned with broadcasting standards, provided the initial leadership in the field of HDTV. Subsequently, this work of the CCIR was assigned to the ITU Radiocommunications Sector (ITU-R) after the reorganization of the ITU in 1993.

The work of the ITU-R in the field of high-definition television was assigned to Study Group 11 (television broadcasting).[1] The assignment was the following:

> *Define* the parameters (digital and analog) of a single HDTV standard for studio production and for the international exchange of HDTV programs.
>
> *Study* the methods of emission of HDTV signals for terrestrial and satellite broadcasting.

The work of Study Group 11 was driven by the recognition that future developments in television services would be of an evolutionary nature and that although it was envisioned that HDTV services would ultimately replace present-day systems, its implementation in some parts of the world could involve intermediate steps or parallel developments such as enhanced television systems.

In 1989, the chairman of Study Group 11 was able to report:

> The CCIR is the only international organization working on HDTV standardization on a worldwide basis. Although the CCIR has dealt with high-definition television since 1972, activities intensified after the XVIth CCIR Plenary Assembly in Dubrovnik (May 1986) to study and to develop HDTV techniques. Studies now cover all aspects of HDTV, both analog and digital: program production, transmission and emission of signals in terrestrial or satellite services, transcoding to the traditional television systems and also the technical links to other existing or forthcoming media. The studies aim at standardization in the interest of the public, of telecommunication administrations and broadcasting organizations.[2]

The work of the ITU-R in HDTV represented a "global approach," taking into account the different delivery media to the consumer, the myriad possible applications of HDTV, and the necessity of harmonization between broadcasting and nonbroadcasting applications of high-resolution imaging. By the end of 1994, the ITU-R had successfully advanced a large portion of the work needed to be done and had made great progress in harmonization between broadcasting and nonbroadcasting applications.

ITU-R develops **Recommendations** (standards and practices) in response to a **Question** or a series of Questions. The primary Questions regarding HDTV are found in Table 7-1.

Table 7-1. Questions Regarding HDTV.

No.	Question	Title
1	Q.27-2/11	Standards for the high-definition studio and for international program exchange.
2	Q.47/11	Standards for high-definition television.
3	Q.52/11	Subjective assessment procedures, for picture quality evaluation in an HDTV environment.
4	Q.69/11	The compatibility of the HDTV standard with existing and future standards.
5	Q.70/11	Effect of display technology on the HDTV standard.
6	Q.71/11	Objective measurement in an overall HDTV environment.
7	Q.109/11	Recording of HDTV programs on cinematographic film for international exchange.
8	Q.110/11	Transfer of HDTV programs to non-broadcast media for domestic use according to IEC and ISO standards.
9	Q.119/11	The harmonization of standards for HDTV between broadcast and non-broadcast applications.
10	Q.121/11	Digital Terrestrial Television Broadcasting.
11	Q.201/11	HDTV still image recording.
12	Q.208/11	Bit rate reduction and associated quality parameters for digital HDTV signals.

IN THE BEGINNING. . .

The effort to develop a new high-definition television service was initiated by a Japanese **Proposal for a New Study Program—High Definition Television**. *CCIR Document 11/31, 17 March 1972.*

In March 1972, the Japanese Administration proposed that the CCIR institute studies on high-definition television services. The proposal noted that the existing television broadcasting services were inferior to motion pictures and printed pictures with regard to sharpness and inferior to high-fidelity sound broadcasting with respect to sound. The proposal noted that a higher-quality television system would be required to meet the future needs for entertainment and educational applications, and envisaged the use of large screen displays. The proposal also suggested that the viewing area aspect ratio (H:V) might lie in the range from 5:3 (1.667:1) to 2:1, with a modulation transfer function of at least 50% at a resolution of 700–900 television lines. The proposal called for a study program to define the requirements for such a system[3] and to determine what standards should be recommended for high-definition television systems intended for broadcasting to the general public.[4]

Work on high-definition television began within the CCIR with the adoption of Question 27/11. The adoption of Question 27/11 subsequently led to a number of Questions, Study Programs, Resolutions, and Decisions regarding HDTV.

Within Study Group 11, two Study Programs were created: 27A/11, concerned with HDTV compatibility with existing standards and broadcast channel assignments; and 27B/11, concerned with display technologies. The study programs led to Decisions which provided a structure for the investigation of this new service. The Decisions included: Decision 58, which established Interim Working Party (IWP) 11/6, charged with the study of HDTV; Decision 60, which charged IWP 11/7 on digital television to investigate the application of digital technology within HDTV; Decision 66, which charged IWP 11/4 on subjective assessments to investigate the means of assessment of HDTV system performance; and Decision 59, establishing a cooperative effort with Study Group 10, to investigate the means of video recording.

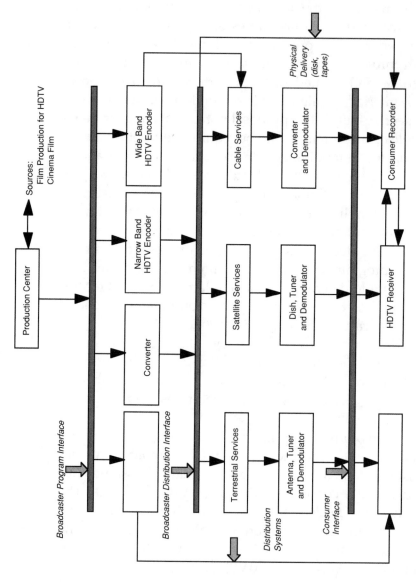

Figure 7-1. HDTV Delivery of Services.

The Study Groups also approved Decision 51 asking for a Joint Interim Working Party (JIWP 10-11/3) on Satellite Broadcasting of HDTV to stimulate studies in this important area of broadcasting distribution.

By 1987, the chairman of Study Group 11 was able to report that the HDTV system being developed represented a leap forward in terms of television broadcasting quality and that it would be radically different from the earlier stages in the development of television technology. The chairman's report[5] stated:

> The special significance of HDTV is that for the first time in the history of television, the viewer at home will be able to watch a large image of near photographic quality. HDTV will also effect a dramatic improvement in television and film technology, with the use of electronic techniques in the production of motion-pictures, and it will find a range of applications in printing, medicine and many other fields. HDTV should therefore be seen as a multi-purpose system of great potential.

By 1987, the international community realized that the success of this new standard was dependent on establishing a future environment for HDTV as it related to broadcasting. An initial study produced a simplified schematic of a global approach to the HDTV environment, based on a suggestion by the chairman of Study Group 11,[6] and is shown in Figure 7-1.[7] In this model, the central element was the HDTV production center serving as the source of programs both for domestic use and for international exchange. Although most programming would be in a high-definition television production format, provision was made for the importing of programming material in other formats both in digital and analog forms, particularly from archival material. One of the stated goals of the HDTV production format was to provide near-35-mm image quality. One application for such a system is the creation of electronic-generated, special-effects image sequences for intercutting with 35-mm film. Therefore, the HDTV production facility was seen as incorporating both high-quality video-to-film transfer processes and film-to-video telecine processes.

The model described the flow of program content to the consumer beginning with HDTV signals that originate in a production center and are then passed to a broadcast distribution network. Delivery to the consumer could be via myriad distribution media such as UHF or VHF terrestrial broadcasting, satellite distribution, cable services, or prerecorded video tape or video disks. The consumer's choice of delivery media could impact the level of performance of the service received. The model provided for delivery of full-bandwidth and wide-band HDTV, narrowband HDTV, enhanced television (EDTV), or improved digitized 525- and 625-line services.

From the standpoint of the continued use of existing television transmission networks and cable television systems, maintaining frequency plans currently in force when introducing HDTV was seen as an important issue. The introduction of narrowband HDTV services in the UHF and VHF bands would be constrained by the nominal bandwidths for the existing standard television channels used throughout the world, namely 6, 7, and 8 MHz.

The HDTV consumer's receiver was seen as having to be able to display any of the services at an appropriate level of performance. Such a receiver could include the necessary signal processing to reconstruct, as accurately as possible, the signal as distributed. The model envisioned that the processing might include display up-conversion, ghost cancellation, noise filtering, and so forth. It was also deemed conceivable that adapters could provide an improved, down-converted service to existing 525- and 625-line receivers.[8]

Studies based on the original Japanese proposal, augmented by an understanding of the flow of programming to the consumer as shown in Figure 7-1, produced an agreement on the basic principles and definition of an HDTV service:

- Spatial resolution in the vertical and horizontal directions of about twice the conventional television systems (referenced to ITU-R Recommendation 601)
- Any worthwhile improvements in temporal resolution beyond that achieved by conventional television systems (referenced to ITU-R Recommendation 601)
- Improved color rendition over that achieved by conventional television systems
- A wider picture aspect ratio (16:9 versus 4:3) as compared to conventional television systems
- Multichannel high-fidelity sound.[9]

Recognizing the importance of data services, in 1985 the chairman of Study Group 11 proposed the development of systems similar to teletext for use in HDTV.[10]

HDTV PRODUCTION TECHNOLOGY

The introduction of a new and superior television system with a goal of equaling the program delivery quality and performance of 35-mm film has great implications. One of the obvious implications is the need for a new production standard equal to the task of supporting the new system. This raised the possibility of developing a production standard that not only meets the broadcasters' requirements for HDTV television production but also meets the needs of the film community for special effects.

The development of an HDTV studio standard was first assigned to Interim Working Party (IWP) 11/6, Mr. Y. Tadakoro (Japan), Chairman, and after the reorganization of Study Group 11 activities in 1990, to Task Group 11/1, Dr. Richard Green (U.S.A.), and since 1994, with Mr. Kenneth Davies (Canada) as chairman.

HDTV production technology was seen from the very beginning as an opportunity to simplify program exchange, bringing together the production of programs for television and for the cinema. The concept of a single production standard serving all regions of the world and with application in the film community clearly could provide benefits to both broadcasting organizations and program producers. All Administrations stated their preference for a single worldwide standard for HDTV studio production and international program exchange.

The task of creating a Recommendation for high-definition television studio production and international program exchange was made somewhat difficult by the diversity of objectives foreseen for HDTV in different parts of the world. There were differences in approach in terms of technology, support systems, and compatibility. It became clear that for some Administrations, the use of HDTV for production of motion pictures and their subsequent distribution via satellites was the most immediate need. For other Administrations, there was a greater emphasis on satellite broadcasting, with a diversity of opinion on both time scale for service introduction and the frequency bands to be used. For still other Administrations, the dominant consideration remained terrestrial broadcasting services.

The proposal for a draft Recommendation for an HDTV studio standard based on a 60-Hz field rate and 1125 total lines was submitted to the CCIR in 1985. Table 7-2 lists the basic characteristics of the video signal for the 1125/60 system. The proposal for a draft Recommendation for an HDTV studio standard based on a 50-Hz field rate and 1250 total lines was submitted to the CCIR in 1987. Table 7-3 lists the basic characteristics of the video signal for the 1250/50 system.

Table 7-2. Basic Characteristics of Video Signals Based on an 1125/60 System.[11]

Item	Characteristics	Value
1	Number of lines per frame	1125
2	Number of picture lines per frame	1035
3	Interlace ratio	2:1
4	Picture aspect ratio (H:V)	16:9
5	Field frequency (fields/s)	60.00
6	Line frequency (Hz)	33,750

Table 7-3. Basic Characteristics of Video Signals Based on a 1250/50 System.[12]

Item	Characteristics	Value
1	Number of lines per frame	1250
2	Number of picture lines per frame	1152
3	Interlace ratio	1:1 (Proscan)
4	Picture aspect ratio (H:V)	16:9
5	Field frequency (fields/s)	50.00
6	Line frequency (Hz)	62,500

Neither set of parameters in those drafts achieved a consensus within the ITU-R as a single worldwide standard. However, both had sufficient support for practical use in specific areas to encourage manufacturers to produce equipment.

In 1994, the Society of Motion Pictures and Television Engineers (SMPTE) at the request of several Administrations including the Asia–Pacific Broadcasting Union,[13] Australia,[14] Canada, New Zealand, and the United States developed a single family of standards with maximum commonality for use in both 50-Hz and 60-Hz environments and also defined for operation at 24-Hz for film applications to ensure minimum degradation in program exchange between countries. This proposal for an HDTV studio standard based on a 1920 x 1080 active scanning structure and providing for both 50- and 60-Hz field rates was submitted to Task Group 11/1.[15] Table 7-4 lists the basic characteristics of the video 1920 x 1080 signal.

Table 7-4. Basic Characteristics of Video Signals Based on a 1080/50 and 1080/60 System.[16, 17]

Item	Characteristics	Values
1	Number of lines per frame	1125
2	Number of picture lines per frame	1080
3	Interlace ratio	2:1 or 1:1
4	Picture aspect ration (H:V)	16:9
5	Field frequency (fields/s)	50.00, 59.94 +, 60.00
6	Line frequency (Hz)	31,250, 33,750

It is important to note that the difficulties in reaching international agreement on a source standard were caused not so much by the different technical levels and economic capabilities of individual countries as by the question of what HDTV services were envisioned and by the specific national view on an implementation plan.[18, 19, 20, 21]

In international studies, there is often a tendency to focus on the points of disagreement rather than the points of agreement. On the positive note, there was much agreement in the area of an HDTV source standard. The specific parameters agreed upon included a picture aspect ratio (16:9) and a single worldwide agreement on both color rendition and on the equation for luminance. For the first time in the history of television, all countries of the world agreed on the technical definition of a basic tristimulus color system for displays. Also agreed upon, in principal, were the digital HDTV bit rate values for the studio interface signal, important to determining both the interface for HDTV transmission and the use of digital recording.

All of these agreements culminated in Recommendation 709, adopted by the XVII Plenary Assembly of the CCIR in 1990 in Dusseldorf.[22] The draft text of this Recommendation was presented by Dr. George Waters (EBU), chair of Working Group 11A during the final meeting of Study Group 11 (October 1989). The draft Recommendation was unanimously approved on 25 October.[23]

Table 7-5. Opto-electronic Conversion.[24]

Item	Parameter	Value		
1.1	Opto-electronic transfer characteristics before nonlinear precorrection.	Assumed linear.		
1.2	Overall opto-electronic transfer characteristics at source.	$V = 1.099\ L^{0.45} - 0.099$ for $1 \geq L \geq 0.018$ $V = 4.500L$ for $0.018 \geq L \geq 0$ where L is the luminance of the image and where $0 \leq L \leq 1$ and V is the corresponding electrical signal.		
1.3	Chromaticity coordinates (CIE 1931): —For reference primaries, see **Note** below. —For interim primaries related to current display technology.	**Primary** Red Green Blue	x 0.6400 0.3000 0.1500	y 0.3300 0.6000 0.0600
1.4	Assumed chromaticity for equal primary signals $E_R = E_G = E_B$ (Reference White)	D_{65} x 0.3127		y 0.3290

Note: Studies to establish parameter values for the reference primary colors, nonlinear video processing, and video matrixing are in progress to improve future display color rendition and to optimize transformation among HDTV, film, graphics, and color hard copy.

This work established the concept of a "reference system" and a set of interim parameter values related to the then-current display technology. The availability of a reference system helped to optimize transformations among HDTV, film, graphics, and color printing. The agreement on the wide aspect ratio display provided for the evolution of compatible wide-screen television systems in those regions of the world which wished to adopt an evolutionary approach toward a single worldwide standard for HDTV. The agreement on the reference system included opto-electronic conversion parameters (Table 7-5), picture characteristics (Table 7-6), picture scanning characteristics (Table 7-7), signal format (Table 7-8), analog representation (Table 7-9), and the digital representation (Table 7-10).

Later studies by the SMPTE Working Group on Production Colorimetry offered revised recommendations on wide-gamut colorimetry which provided for the processing of negative RGB signals.[25] These studies recognized that the color coding used to date limited the capture and transmission of the color gamut to that of the phosphors used in monitors and displays. However, future displays may provide reproduction of a wider, richer color gamut. The SMPTE recommended allowing the reproduction of the Pointer Maximum Surface Colors as described by M.R. Pointer in 1980. The SMPTE recommendation included the reference primaries for RGB (Red, Green, Blue) described in Table 7-5, assuming white reflectance of 90% for computation of the RGB signal levels. The range of linear RGB signal levels to reproduce all the Pointer colors is then $-22\% \le RGB \le 133\%$. This leads to changes in the equations for gamma-corrected luminance (Y):

$$Y = 1.099L^{0.045} - 0.099 \qquad \text{for } 0.018 \le L \le 1.33,$$

$$Y = 4.5L \qquad \text{for } -0.0045 \le L \le 0.018,$$

$$Y = -[1.099(-4L)^{0.45} - 0.099]/4 \qquad \text{for } -0.250 \le L \le -0.0045.$$

Table 7-6. Picture Characteristics.[26]

Item	Parameter	Value
2.1	Aspect ratio	16:9
2.2	Samples per active line	1920
2.3	Sampling lattice	Orthogonal

Table 7-7. Picture Scanning Characteristics.[27]

Item	Parameter	Value
3.1	Order of sample scanning	Left to right, top to bottom
3.2	Interlace ratio	See **Note** below.

Note: The objective for the system is defined to be progressive scanning (1:1 interlace ratio). For current implementations, an interlace ratio of 2:1 or an equivalent sample-rate reduction process may be used.

Some important parameters relating to picture characteristics and picture scanning characteristics still remained to be agreed upon. A number of concepts were proposed that might have formed the basis for a worldwide standard. These included the Common Image Format (CIF),[28] the Common Data Rate (CDR),[29] the Common Image Part (CIP), and the Common Sampling Lattice (CSL) proposals, the latter two providing a combination of the benefits of the CIF and CDR approaches.

Table 7-8. Signal Format.

Item	Parameter	Value
4.1	Conceptual nonlinear precorrection of primary signals.	$\gamma = 0.45$
4.2	Derivation of luminance signal E'_Y: —Equation for interim systems related to reference primaries; see **Note** below. —Equation for interim systems related to current display technology and conventional coding.	$E'_Y = 0.2125\, E'_R +$ $0.7154\, E'_G +$ $0.0721\, E'_B$
4.3	Derivation of color-difference signals (analog coding), E'_{PB}; E'_{PR}: —Equation for system related to reference primaries; see **Note** below. —Equation for interim systems related to current display technology and conventional coding.	$E'_{PB} = 0.5389\,(E'_B - E'_Y)$ $E'_{PR} = 0.6349\,(E'_R - E'_Y)$
4.4	Derivation of color-difference signals (digital coding) C_1, C_2.	Digitally scaled from the values of 4.3.

Note: Studies to establish the parameter values for the luminance and color-difference equations are in progress to improve system performance and optimize transformations among HDTV, film graphics, and color hard copy.

These approaches were an attempt to find a "unified" approach to a single standard, recognizing that the development of a single unique standard was constrained by the desire for compatibility with the frame rates of the conventional television systems at 50-Hz and 59.94-Hz field rates. It was foreseen that such constraints would likely be removed, in time, by developments in technology leading to a standard based on a higher frame rate for better motion rendition or digital receivers with memory that were field/frame rate agile.

Table 7-9. Analog Representation.

Item	Parameter	Value (mV)
5.1	Nominal level—E'_R, E'_G, E'_B, E'_Y	Ref. Black—0 Ref. White—700
5.2	Nominal level—E'_{PB}, E'_{PR}	± 350
5.3	Format of synchronizing signals	Trilevel bipolar (see Figure 7-2)
5.4	Timing reference	(See Figure 7-2)
5.5	Sync level	300 Sync on all components (See Figure 7-3)

Table 7-10. Digital Representation.

Item	Parameter	Value
6.1	Coded signals	R, G, B or Y, C_1, C_2
6.2	Sampling lattice R, G, B, Y	Orthogonal line, and picture repetitive.
6.3	Sampling lattice C_1, C_2	Samples cosited with each other and with alternate luminance samples.
6.4	Sampling frequency R, G, B, Y	Sampling frequency is an integer multiple of 2.25 MHz.
6.5	Sampling frequency C_1, C_2	Color-difference sampling frequency to be $(1/2)Y$ times sampling frequency.

The CIF approach suggested use of common values for parameters defining the active picture area in different HDTV system implementations. In this approach, the image space was a bounded, two-dimensional representation of three-dimensional space in which a common set of spatial characteristics and luminance and color transfer functions are shared by all variations of the standard, as shown in Figure 7-4.

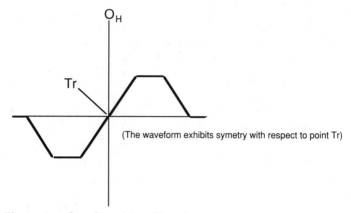

Figure 7-2. Synchronizing Signal.

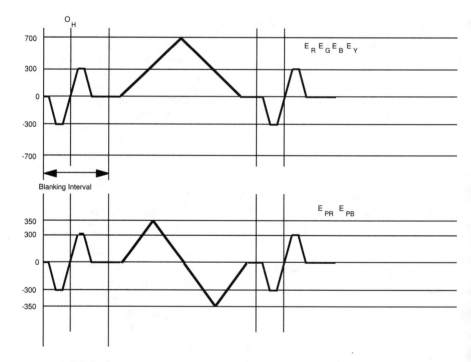

Figure 7-3. Component Signal Levels.

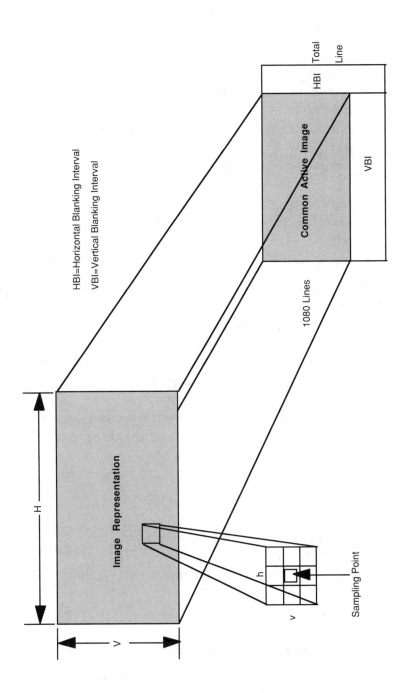

HBI=Horizontal Blanking Interval

VBI=Vertical Blanking Interval

Image Representation

Common Active Image

1080 Lines

Total Line

HBI

VBI

Sampling Point

Figure 7-4. Common Image Format.

The CIF approach implied a worldwide agreement on the following basic parameters:

- Aspect ratio of the image
- Aspect ratio of the picture element (pel)
- Number of active samples in the horizontal direction
- Number of active samples (lines) in the vertical direction
- Sample arrangement (orthogonal)
- Opto-electronic transfer characteristic at the camera
- Colorimetry, reference primaries, and reference white
- Electro-optic transfer characteristic at the display.

The blanking periods, total line period, and the total number of lines would be varied among members of the family to provide compatibility with existing picture rates.

The CDR approach was based on CCIR Recommendation 601 and recognized that although differing values for parameters defining the active picture area in different HDTV system implementations may need to be accommodated, the values chosen can lead to a common data rate. The CDR approach implied a worldwide agreement on the following basic parameters:

- Aspect ratio of the image
- Number of active samples in the horizontal direction
- Sample arrangement (orthogonal)
- Sampling rate and data rate
- Opto-electronic transfer characteristic at the camera
- Colorimetry, reference primaries, and reference white
- Electro-optic transfer characteristic at the display.

The blanking periods, aspect ratio of the picture element (pel), total line period, and the number of active lines as well as the total number of lines could be varied among members of the CDR family to provide compatibility with existing picture rates.

Also proposed was the possibility of combining the CIF and CDR approaches by enclosing the proposed CIF active image structure within a full-frame structure through the use of different but realistic values for horizontal and vertical blanking. The data samples that exist in the horizontal and vertical blanking periods in the digital version of the standard would differ in number and could be utilized for additional sound channels and to meet other data capacity requirements. The CSL concept provided a possible path to the harmonization of formats between different image applications. Such an approach becomes realistic with the presence of a frame buffer memory at a number of points in production delivery chains. A digital solution provides a fundamental change in the way the question of standardizing the HDTV picture and scanning parameters can be addressed.

Consideration of the possible use of HDTV displays for computers leads to the examination of criteria common to both fields of activity. Taking account of these findings was seen as critical to the development of synergy between HDTV production and related computer applications in the near term and the HDTV consumer display and personal computer equipment in the long term. The effort to further harmonize the relationship between HDTV production and related computer applications in the near term also resulted in consideration of square sample distribution[30] and square pels.[31]

The 1080-line system described in Table 7-4 meets the requirements for both CIF and CDR approaches as well as providing for square pels.

Recognizing that the long-term future of HDTV lies in the application of digital technology and in the establishment of unique worldwide standards, the ITU-R investigated various paths to implementing a digital solution.

One possible path involved the concept of *the virtual studio standard*. This concept provided for a unique digital data bus used to transport and record HDTV signals. The source and destination communicate by using a unified data format through gateways which perform any required standards conversion. The virtual studio standard general characteristics include the following:

1. Operation in the digital domain, because of flexibility and processing capability required
2. Independence from the physical studio equipment and therefore from the current state of technology
3. Headroom for production, standards conversion, and future needs
4. Manageable bit rates
5. Minimizing of artifacts resulting from possible conversions.[32]

During the 1986–1990 study period, studies were initiated on integrating teletext and other data broadcasting services into HDTV systems, consideration of suitable sound systems were begun in cooperation with ITU-R Study Group 10 (responsible for sound broadcasting) chaired by Mr. Carlo Terzani (Italy), and transmission of HDTV signals in communication links were begun in cooperation with CMTT, chaired by Mr. W.G. Simpson (United Kingdom). The work of the CMTT was continued after the 1993 reorganization of the ITU by ITU-T Study Group 9, chaired by Mr. José Luis Tejerina (Spain).

The ITU-R efforts in the area of studio production and international program exchange are documented in Recommendation 709.[33, 34, 35, 36]

HDTV Transmission: Phase 1–Analog Technology

The ability to transmit HDTV images to the consumer was demonstrated, first in Japan, and then in Europe, using analog transmission technology with the primary transmission media being direct broadcast satellite.

Progress toward the development of HDTV analog transmission was first reported in the work of the Interim Working Party (IWP) 11/6, Mr. Y. Tadakoro (Japan), chairman, and after the reorganization of Study Group 11 activities in 1990, in the work of Task Group 11/1, Dr. Richard Green (U.S.A.), chairman, and focused on two systems, the MUSE and the HD-MAC.

The study of high-definition television with respect to satellite broadcasting fell to the Joint Interim Working Party (JIWP) 10-11/3, chaired by Mr. Ö. Mäkitalo (Sweden), working with IWP 11/6. JIWP 10-11/3 was charged with investigating HDTV from the point of view of satellite broadcasting with respect to three possible implementations: narrow-RF(radio-frequency)-band systems using frequency modulation (FM) technology, wide-RF-band systems using FM, and digitally modulated systems.

JIWP 10-11/3 identified techniques for the broadcasting of high-definition television by satellite over a range of frequencies up to about 23 GHz. The techniques employed included bandwidth reduction, channel coding, multiplexing, modulation, and reception. The studies carried out by JIWP 10-11/3 indicated that the RF parameters and the need for sharing placed constraints on the emission format. However, neither the characteristics of satellite broadcasting systems nor their interference susceptibility were seen as directly restricting the characteristics of the studio standard used for the source programs. JIWP 10-11/3 noted that the 12-GHz bands provided for satellite broadcasting using channel widths of 24 MHz in Region 2 and 27 MHz in Regions 1 and 3. In order to transmit high-definition television within these channels, the source signals had to be reduced in bandwidth from either 60-MHz bandwidth analog signals or 1.2-Gbits/s digital signals through extensive signal processing. Two narrow RF-band systems (MUSE, HD-MAC) designed for the narrowband satellite broadcasting environment provided such signal compression at the expense of some reduction in the resolution of areas of the picture exhibiting motion.[37]

Although characteristics of several systems had been reported to the ITU-R, the work on the MUSE and HD-MAC systems was not only more extensive than other proposals but was brought to the point of practice.

The MUSE system[38] was developed in Japan for broadcasting of an HDTV service using a single planned satellite channel. The system employed both spatial and temporal subsampling techniques (4:1 dot-interlaced subsampling which employs interfield and interframe offsets) to achieve reduction in required bandwidth. The baseband signal bandwidth is 8.1 MHz. Motion-compensation techniques were applied for the purpose of improving the effect of subsampling in the case of uniform movement in the picture and effectively uses the properties of the human visual system. A technique for analog-sampled value transmission was used including automatic waveform equalization at the encoder and receiver. Sound and data signals were inserted into the field blanking period for transmission. The baseband multiplexing system was designed to accommodate the requirements of cable distribution systems as well as the satellite transmission environment.

The HD-MAC system[39] was developed in Europe in the context of the EUREKA-95 project and utilized time-division multiplex techniques. The system was designed for use in satellite broadcasting and in any transmission medium which guarantees a baseband of 11 MHz. The system employed three luminance/temporal coding branches all using a quincunx subsampling lattice. The three branches were the following: an 80-ms branch with HDTV resolution for stationary areas, a 40-ms motion-compensated branch for velocities up to 12 samples per 40 ms, and a 20-ms branch for rapid motion and sudden picture changes except when in the film mode. Sound and data signals were coded according to the MAC/packet specification. The characteristics of the MUSE and HD-MAC systems are summarized in Table 7-11.

Table 7-11. Characteristics of Example HDTV Satellite Broadcasting Systems.[40]

Parameter	MUSE	HD-MAC
Picture aspect ratio	16:9	16:9
Picture rate	30	25
Scanning structure (lines/fields/interlace)	1125/60/2:1	1250/50/2:1
Active lines/picture	1032	1152
Sampling frequency (MHz)	Y:44.55/C:14.85	54
Active samples/line: Luminance Color difference	1122 376	1440 720
Type of coding	Analog	Analog
Compression method	Motion-adaptive subsampling	Motion-adaptive subsampling
Maximum luminance bandwidth (MHz)	22	21
Maximum color-difference bandwidth (MHz)	7	10.5
Luminance subsampling (horizontal)	3:1	2:1
Color-difference subsampling (horizontal)	4:1	2:1
Color-difference subsampling (vertical)	2:1	2:1
Luminance compression	12:11	3:2
Color-difference compression	48:11	3:1

Table 7-11. (continued)

Parameter	MUSE	HD-MAC
Transmitted base bandwidth (MHz)	8.1	10.125
Digital assistance (Mbits/s)	—	1–2
Digital sound/data multiplex (Mbits/s)	1.35	1.5–3.0
Sound signal bandwidth (kHz)	20 or 15	15
Sound sampling frequency (kHz)	48/32	32
Coding/modulation method	DPCM/ternary	PCM/duobinary
Companding law	16:11, 6 ranges	14–10 NICAM
Digital time compression	13.5:1	6.6:1
Number of sound channels	2/4	2/4/8
Type of modulation and deviation (MHz)	FM/10.2	FM/9.55
Required bandwidth (MHz)	21–24	27

The possibility of terrestrial television broadcasting of high-definition television was reviewed during the 1986–1990 CCIR study period. Three of the existing Interim Working Parties, IWP 11/5 chaired by Mr. S. Dinsel (Germany), IWP 11/6 chaired by Mr. Y. Tadakoro, and IWP 11/7 chaired by Mr. A.N. Heightman (United Kingdom), worked together to produce early guidelines.

Specifically, IWP 11/5 produced a progress report of a general nature on protection ratios applicable to HDTV used in terrestrial broadcasting and on compatibility of HDTV systems with existing terrestrial services including cable distribution. IWP 11/5 tentatively concluded that the protection-ratio figures for existing 525-line and 625-line television systems, especially in the case of cable transmission, would cover the requirements for high-definition television in many cases. IWP 11/6 was charged with investigating the sensitivity against interference in the case of the bandwidth compression of the data/sound portions of the signal which were seen as probably being digital. The contribution of IWP 11/7 resulted in a report giving some detailed information on the choice of parameters for a digital version of the production standard, leading to the question of whether there was a possibility for creating a digital terrestrial television broadcasting (DTTB) system.[41]

After the reorganization of the CCIR structure in 1990, the work of IWP 11/7 on digital coding was continued in Working Party 11B chaired by Mr. T. Nishizawa (Japan), the work of IWP 11/5 on planning factors was continued in Working Party 11/C chaired by Mr. S. Prepar (Slovenia), the work on data broadcasting was continued in Working Party 11/D chaired by Professor F. Cappuccini (Italy), and the work of IWP 11/7 on digital interfaces was continued in Task Group 11/2 chaired by Mr. D. Nasse (France).

HDTV TRANSMISSION: PHASE 2–DIGITAL TECHNOLOGY

The application of digital technology in the various television disciplines began in the early 1970s with the introduction of digital graphics machines and digital video processing devices. By 1990, efforts in North America to find a means of transmitting a HDTV image within the existing 6-MHz bandwidth, VHF, and UHF television channels focused on the use of digital data compression and modulation schemes to meet system requirements. Practical feasibility demonstrations of different systems in North America were quickly followed by similar demonstrations in Europe and Japan.

By mid-1991, publications reporting on work being done in the United States, in the Nordic countries, in the United Kingdom, in France, and in other parts of the world showed that bit-rate reduction schemes on the order of

60:1 could be successfully applied to HDTV source images. The results of this work implied that HDTV image sequences could be transmitted in a relatively narrow narrowband channel in the range of 15–25 Mbits/s. Using standard, proven modulation technologies, it would therefore be possible to transmit an HDTV program within the existing 6-, 7-, and 8-MHz channel bandwidths provided for in the VHF and UHF television bands.

As a result, during 1991, various Administrations requested that the chairman of Study Group 11 initiate a study concerning the issue of digital terrestrial television broadcasting. This led to the establishment, in November 1991, of an ad hoc group, chaired by Mr. K.P. Davies (Canada), then vice-chairman of Task Group 11/1, to discuss the various proposals and to provide a report on possible action to be taken. This ad hoc group presented its results in the form of a new Question to be urgently approved and assigned to a new Task Group on Digital Terrestrial Television Broadcasting (TG11/3).

Due to the urgency of the studies and the need to establish Task Group 11/3 as soon as possible, the Administration of Australia accepted the invitation of the meeting to immediately endorse a new Question and propose it for adoption by correspondence according to rule No. 326 of the Nairobi Convention. Administrative Circular number 340 was mailed to all Administrations and received support by more than the necessary administrations in January 1992. The chairman of Study Group 11, in consultation with the director of CCIR, Mr. R. Kirby, established Task Group 11/3 with Mr. S. Baron (U.S.A.) as its chairman.

The work of Task Group 11/3 involved developing the relevant technical parameters such as source coding, channel coding, modulation, spectrum utilization, and protection from interference. Therefore, the work of Task Group 11/3 was seen as structured on a project basis with a charge to develop a total system rather than providing Recommendations and Reports on a specific area of specialty. The concept of project-oriented assignments represented the new thrust of the ITU as a means of proceeding on urgent Questions. The work of Task Group 11/3 forms the majority of the body of this book.

EXTREMELY HIGH-RESOLUTION IMAGERY

By 1994, the world community had established interest in images for other applications with resolutions exceeding the approximately 1000 lines chosen for the HDTV system. ITU-R Working Party 11F proposed[42] a hierarchy of digital spatial resolution models based on the 1920(H) x 1080(V) square pixel structure. Four levels were proposed for the model:

Level	Spatial Resolution
HRI-0	1920x1080
HRI-1	3840x2160
HRI-2	5760x3240
HRI-3	7680x4320

The hierarchy assumes screen aspect ratios of 16:9, and the temporal resolution may be "still," non-real time, or real time at frame rates appropriate to the application. For real-time events, a system of approximately 60 frames/s or higher using progressive scan appears to be appropriate. Image coding levels at 8 bits for moving images and 10 bits for still images were considered desirable, with 12-bit coding levels used for image manipulation and processing.

One of the most intensive uses of these high-resolution image systems is in digital film–optical effects and other forms of electronic processing of films such as restoration work. Uses to date have included compositing with computer-generated graphics, retouching of scenes to remove unwanted portions of the landscape or replacement of portions of the landscape, changing color, and even insertion or deletion of actors and actresses into or from scenes. The film applications are non-real time applications and the technology required to support these applications at the HRI-0 level is currently available. The HRI-0 level is considered marginally acceptable for use with 35-mm film. Projections on the ability to support the high-resolution imaging levels in real time with technology are provided in Table 7-12.

Table 7-12. Technology Required to Support High-resolution Imaging.

Item	HRI-0	HRI-1	HRI-2	HRI-3
A/D converter	Mass production 1994–1995	Realization expected 1997	Difficult, technology breakthrough required	Breakthrough required
D/A converter	Mass production possible	Trial production levels	Realization expected 1997	Realization expected 2000
Maximum sampling frequency	<150 MHz	<500 MHz	<1200 MHz	<2000 MHz
Frame memory requirement	40-Mbits. Mass production possible	165-Mbits. Trial production	670-Mbits. Realization expected 2000	1.2-Gbits. Realization expected 2003
LSI processing	0.5 μm, possible	0.35μm, in trial production	0.25-Mbit. Realization expected 2000	0.15-Mbit. Realization expected 2003
Encoder logic:	6M transistors:	12M transistors:	30M transistors:	100M transistors:
1 Chip—LSI	Possible	Possible with new architectures	Breakthrough required	Breakthrough required
1 Chip—DSP	Special VLSI	Breakthrough required	Breakthrough required	Breakthrough required
Decoder logic:	2M transistors:	5M transistors:	12M transistors:	30M transistors:
1 Chip—LSI	Possible	May be possible	May be possible, new architecture	Breakthrough required
1 Chip—DSP	Special VLSI chip	May be possible	Breakthrough required	Breakthrough required

END NOTES

1. Study Group 11 is assigned responsibility for all aspects of television broadcasting, including conventional (i.e., NTSC, PAL, and SECAM) and enhanced systems, as well as the international exchange of all types of television programs.

2. CCIR Document 11/290-E, "Preliminary Report of the Chairman of Study Group 11 to the Extraordinary Meeting of Study Group 11 on HDTV," 8 February 1989, p. 2.

3. CCIR Document 11/31-E, "Proposal for a New Study Program—High-Definition Television," 17 March 1972.

4. Corr. 1 to CCIR Doc. 11/31-E, 7 July 1972.

5. CCIR Document 11/134-E, "Report by the Chairman of Study Group 11 (Broadcasting Service [Television]) to the Interim Meeting of Study Group 11," 5 October 1987, pp. 1–2.

6. CCIR Document 11/173, November 1987, p. 3.

7. CCIR Report 801-3, "The Present State of High-Definition Television," June 1989, Figure 1.

8. CCIR Report 801-3, "The Present State of High-Definition Television," June 1989, pp. 17–19.

9. CCIR Report 801-3, "The Present State of High-Definition Television," June 1989, p. 22.

10. CCIR Document 11/485, "Summary Record of the Third Meeting," 28 October 1985, p. 2.

11. CCIR Report 801-3, "The Present State of High-Definition Television," June 1989, p. 37.

12. CCIR Report 801-3, "The Present State of High-Definition Television," June 1989, p. 46.

13. ITU Document 11-1/17, Asia–Pacific Broadcasting Union, "HDTV Studio Standard," 10 October 1994.

14. ITU-R Document 11-1/9, "Standards for Digital HDTV Studios," 13 September 1994.

15. Document 11-1/19, "Proposed SMPTE Standard for Television 1920 x 1080 Scanning and Interface," 10 October 1994.

16. SMPTE 274, "SMPTE Standard—for Television—1920 x 1080 Scanning and Interface."

17. SMPTE S17.395, "Proposed SMPTE Standard—for Television—1920 x 1080-50 Hz—Scanning and Interface."

18. R.L. Nickelson, "The Evolution of HDTV in the Work of the CCIR," *IEEE Transactions on Broadcasting*, Vol. 35, III (1989), 250–259.

19. R. Hopkins, and K.P. Davies, "Development of HDTV Emission Systems in North America," *IEEE Transactions on Broadcasting*, Vol. 35, III (1989), 259–270.

20. M. Hatori, and Y. Nakamura, "1125/60 HDTV Studio Standard Intended to Be a Worldwide Unified HDTV Standard," *IEEE Transactions on Broadcasting*, Vol. 35, III (1989), 270–279.

21. N. Wassiczek, G.T. Waters, and D. Wood, "European Perspectives on HDTV Studio Production Standards," *IEEE Transactions on Broadcasting*, Vol. 35, III (1989), 279.

22. CCIR Document PLEN/69 (Rev. 2)-E, "Minutes of the Third Plenary Meeting," 29 May 1990, pp. 2–4.

23. CCIR Document 11/745, 25 November 1989, p. 6.

24. CCIR Document 11/1007 (Rev. 1)-E, "Basic Parameter Values for the HDTV Standard for the Studio and for International Program Exchange," 24 May 1990, p. 3.

25. CCIR Report 1217, "Future Development of HDTV," 1990. pp. 1–2.

26. CCIR Document 11/1007 (Rev. 1)-E, "Basic Parameter Values for the HDTV Standard for the Studio and for International Program Exchange," 24 May 1990, p. 4.

27. ITU-R Document 11-1/18, "SMPTE Recommendation for HDTV Wide-Gamut Colorimetry," 10 October 1994.

28. Common image format is based on the definition of a common image structure that can be used in systems that have different frame rates or even different scanning methods. The common elements include picture aspect ratio, number of *active* lines, number of active pixels per line, colorimetry, and transfer characteristics.

29. Common data rate standards would be adopted with a common data rate shared by implementations with differing line and field rates but providing a maximum commonality in the other parameters, such as line frequency and sampling frequency based on the principles of CCIR Recommendation 601 (Encoding parameters for digital television for studios). Colorimetry and transfer characteristics would also be common.

30. A square sample distribution results when the sampling points are equispaced on the orthogonal horizontal–vertical lattice on a time-discrete image plane.

31. A square pel has equal size in the horizontal and vertical dimensions.

32. CCIR Report 1217, "Future Development of HDTV," 1990, pp. 1–2.

33. M.I. Krivocheev, International trends in HDTV, 27th Electronic Industry Technical Conference, Tokyo, 5 October 1990.

34. F. Cappuccini, and M.I. Krivocheev, "An Outlook on HDTV Standardization," *Telettra Review*, No. 45 (1990).

35. R. Nickelson, "HDTV Standards—Understanding the Issues," *ITU Telecommunication Journal*, 57, V (1990).

36. M.I. Krivocheev, "Current CCIR Activities in HDTV," *ITU Telecommunication Journal*, 58, X (1991).

37. CCIR Document 11/290-E, "Preliminary Report of the Chairman of Study Group 11 to the Extraordinary Meeting of Study Group 11 on HDTV," 8 February 1989, pp. 10–11.

38. Ninomiya et al., Concept of the MUSE system and its protocol, NHK Laboratory Note 348, July 1987.

39. Vreeswijk et al., "HD-MAC Coding of High-Definition Television Signals" (Philips Netherlands, France, U.K.), IEE Conference Publication No. 293, 1988 International Broadcasting Convention, Brighton, U.K.; IEEE Press, New York, 1988.

40. CCIR Report 801-4, "The Present State of High-Definition Television," 1990.

41. CCIR Document 11/290-E, "Preliminary Report of the Chairman of Study Group 11 to the Extraordinary Meeting of Study Group 11 on HDTV," 8 February 1989, pp. 5–7.

42. ITU-R Document 11F/24, "Progress Report on Extremely High-resolution Imagery," 17 October 1994.

8

Advanced Television Services

The service flexibility provided by a digital terrestrial television system with its use of packets of digital data, each packet having a header describing the packet contents, allows the multiplexing of different services into a single channel. The number and quality of the services is dependent only on the data capacity of the channel. This system flexibility has led to the consideration of various types of television services. The prospects for a digital HDTV television service were discussed in the previous chapter. This chapter describes investigations into widescreen services, multiple-program services, and stereoscopic services.

INTRODUCTION

Advanced television services are digital services that provide an enhanced viewing experience over the existing 525-line and 625-line conventional, standard television services. Some of these advanced television services may not necessarily reach the performance level of high-definition television (HDTV). The development of advanced television services is likely to be different from country to country due to various factors which may reflect the availability of spectrum, telecommunications policy, cultural traditions, social and economic considerations, or the state of industrial development. There has been substantial development in the fields of widescreen television services and stereoscopic television services in the last 10 years. The various levels of services from HDTV to LDTV (limited-definition television) are defined in Table 8-1 in terms of such factors as expected viewing distance and picture aspect ratio. Any of the various quality levels of television services could be provided in stereoscopic form.

Table 8-1. Relative Quality of Television Systems.

Characteristic	HDTV[a]	EDTV[a]	SDTV[a]	LDTV[a]
Design viewing distance[b]	3H	4H	6H	8H
Picture Aspect Ratio	16:9	16:9	4:3	4:3

Notes:

(a) HDTV= high-definition television;
   EDTV = enhanced-definition television;
   SDTV = standard-definition television
        = NTSC, PAL, or SECAM;
   LDTV = limited-definition television < VHS quality;

(b) The viewing distance as a multiple of picture height of the display, assuming a subjective assessment score of 100%.

The period between 1990 and 1995 saw rapid development in advanced television services. On 25 November 1991, NHK began regular programming service of the Japanese analog 1125-line MUSE system. In February 1992, the European HD-MAC standard was used at the Olympic Games in Albertville, France. Digital HDTV transmission carried in a standard television broadcasting channel was demonstrated in March 1992. The feasibility of multiprogram television was shown on 21 August 1992 with the simultaneous transmission of two digitally compressed NTSC programs in one satellite channel linking New Jersey in the United States with Moscow via a Russian satellite transponder. During the following month, simulcasting of a digital HDTV service on one channel with standard NTSC service on another channel was successfully demonstrated in the United States at the National Broadcasting Company's (NBC) local broadcasting facility (WRC) in Washington, D.C.

MULTIPROGRAM SERVICES

Standard digital component television sources (525-line/625-line) such as those defined by ITU-R BT.601 offer significant improvements in image performance over services delivered by conventional analog methods (NTSC, PAL, and SECAM). The improvements include elimination of cross-color and cross-luminance artifacts and increased resolution, contributing to a considerably improved picture. These component image sequences can be coded by a digital terrestrial television broadcasting (DTTB) service and compressed into a data stream that uses only a fraction of the channel data space.

The application of digital signal compression technology to coding conventional television signals allows accommodation of multiprogram transmission in the existing 6-, 7-, or 8-MHz channels [multiprogram television (MPTV) 6-7-8 concept].[1,2] Compressed digital television systems offer the prospect of considerable improvement in service quality while appreciably improving spectrum utilization as compared with analog transmission methods. One way of exploiting these possibilities would be to use the bit stream available in digital terrestrial or satellite broadcasting to deliver to the public a certain number of digitally compressed conventional television programs instead of a single conventional, enhanced- or high-definition program. These digitally compressed television signals would be accompanied by digital high-quality sound, coded conditional access information, and ancillary data channels. The European Digital Video Broadcasting (DVB) project has paid particular attention to constructing a digital architecture that could accommodate both HDTV and conventional television services and was interoperable over terrestrial broadcasting, cable, and satellite media. The DVB work led to a series of integrated European telecommunications standards covering digital broadcasting systems,[3] cable,[4] and satellite systems.[5,6] The DVB approach provides harmonization among services by using a unified, common method of video and audio source coding and a unified, common service multiplex and transport. This unified transport data stream is then provided with a framing structure, error protection mechanism, and modulation scheme appropriate to the distribution media. The common transport is seen as a "container" and facilitates the interoperability of the signal through different delivery media. This results in a common data stream after demodulation in the receiver, which simplifies the complexity of the receiving device or appliance. Studies conducted by ITU-R Working Party 10-11S support this container approach and further suggest that the same framing, synchronization, randomization, inner and outer coding, and interleaving mechanisms be applied to all media.[7]

WIDE-SCREEN SERVICES

Enhanced television systems have been developed for both the 525-line and 625-line environments. These television systems attempt to provide a wide-screen service using hybrid analog/digital schemes that are based on and compatible with the existing analog systems.[8] These services are supported by digital wide-screen production formats which can also be used to support EDTV wide-screen DTTB services. The SMPTE has developed a range of wide-screen production formats appropriate for various applications at 483 active lines, both interlaced[9] and progressively[10] scanned images and for 720 active line images.[11] Various organizations within Europe have developed wide-screen formats for 625-line services.[12] Any of these formats can be encoded at an appropriate MPEG-2 profile and level and displayed on an appliance capable of handling that profile/level combination or a higher profile or level.

STEREOSCOPIC TELEVISION

The terms *stereoscopic television* and *three-dimensional television* are often used interchangeably. However, the ITU-R recognizes that these terms are not directly equivalent, and stereoscopic television is recognized as one means of realization of a three-dimensional television service. Three-dimensional television is defined by the ITU-R as television in "which binocular viewing of the television display reproduces the three-dimensional appearance of the scene," whereas stereoscopic television is defined as television in "which separate pictures are presented to each eye so as to reproduce the three-dimensional appearance of the scene."[13] The means of providing stereoscopic television has been under study in various parts of the world. In 1958, Study Group 11 met in Moscow, where the U.S.S.R. submitted a proposal for a new study program on stereoscopic television.[14] A Study Program (11/17) to consider a system of stereoscopic television was approved at the meeting of Study Group 11 in May 1958. Many of the techniques developed in the period through 1992 were proven only in experimental closed-circuit distribution environments and were not necessarily shown to be appropriate for mass-media transmission. The transmission of stereoscopic television pictures required the simultaneous or successive transmission of several signals. Because a practical implementation must make use of an increasingly rarer resource, the spectrum, various methods of bandwidth reduction were investigated.

The chairman of Study Group 11 suggested consideration of holographic technology in lieu of dependence on stereoscopic spectacles as the basis for a new system and requested that studies be conducted on the possible use of holography for this application. He noted that technology can move rapidly and cited the progress made in developing HDTV technology since 1972 as an example.[15]

The ITU-R has stipulated that a practical stereoscopic television system requires the following:[16]

1. Orthoscopic three-dimensional display (the depth of the scene should appear natural and without viewer discomfort)
2. Group viewing (almost any location in the room should provide good stereoscopic viewing)
3. Compatibility (three-dimensional receivers should display stereoscopic transmission in full depth and a two-dimensional transmission monoscopically; existing two-dimensional receivers should display a stereoscopic transmission monoscopically)
4. Nondegraded picture (colorimetry and resolution of a stereoscopic service should be comparable to a conventional service)
5. Minimum modification of video standards (existing specifications should not require extensive revision)
6. Moderate price.

An experimental field sequential stereoscopic television system was developed in Japan utilizing HDTV equipment. Tests results showed that the required field frequency for stereoscopic television was greater than 110 Hz. A system with a field rate of 120 Hz was demonstrated in 1989.[17]

The application of the techniques standardized in the MPEG-2 system lend themselves to efficient coding of stereoscopic television. Assume two cameras viewing a scene, spaced and timed appropriately to allow generation of a stereoscopic television service, and, further, that the output of both cameras conforms to ITU.RB 601. One of the two channels could be compressed as a standard television service at a quality level representing, perhaps, 8.0 Mbits/s. The other channel could be compressed by comparing it with the first channel on a frame-by-frame basis and processing the difference information. Picture information representing image content at a distance in the background would show little or no difference and only foreground information would be retained in the difference frame. The differences between like items in the two channels, spatially displaced due to the stereoscopic effect, could be represented by displacement vectors. Displacement vectors are similar in concept to motion vectors described in current DTTB work. It would appear that the data required to support a frame of displacement vectors is far lower than that required to support the pel data. Working Party 11A prepared a draft Recommendation on Stereoscopic Television based on right-eye and left-eye two-channel signals which establishes a general framework of user requirements dealing with eye fatigue, compatibility with monoscopic displays, and the displacement or disparity signal.[18]

DATA SERVICES

Advanced television service providers can take advantage of the flexibility of the digital transport to provide new and improved data services to the viewers. The broadcaster will be able to provide considerably larger data streams of various types of digital information in a cost-effective way to meet the needs of both the viewing public and the business user.

Data space in the channel that is not assigned to the primary audio and video television services can be assigned to data services. Advanced television data services can include service and program information data, navigational guides, and multimedia services.

Service and program data provide information on the relation between the service (program channel) and the individual program events, program descriptive information such as the name, description, start time and duration, and other information useful to the consumer in program selection, conditional access information, and so forth.[19]

Navigational guides are the mechanism by which the consumer will access the multitude of programs available at any given moment. Given the nature of the DTTB service, this number will be in the hundreds.

The inherent flexibility of DTTB systems using packets of data with headers allows the exchange of multimedia information related to education and training programs and business applications, as well as entertainment. Multimedia services may take many forms: as an entertainment or information television program, a recorded audio document, a teletext page, a computer program, a movie, and so on. All of these forms of information can be accommodated by the DTTB system.

END NOTES

1. M. Krivocheev, "Television and Nothing But Television," *Cinema and Television Technology*, Nos. 10/11 (1991).

2. CCIR Document 11/122, "Report of the Chairman," 31 March 1992, p. 3.

3. European Telecommunications Draft Standard, prETS 300 468, "Digital Broadcasting Systems for Television, sound, and Data Services; Specification for Service Information (SI) in Digital Video Broadcasting (DVB) Systems," November 1994.

4. European Telecommunications Draft Standard, prETS 300 429, "Digital Broadcasting Systems for Television, Sound and Data Services; Framing Structure, Channel Coding, and Modulation: Cable Systems," August 1994.

5. European Telecommunications Draft Standard, prETS 300 421, "Digital Broadcasting Systems for Television, Sound and Data Services; Framing Structure, Channel Coding, and Modulation for 11/12 GHz Satellite Services," August 1994.

6. European Telecommunications Draft Report, ETR 154, "Digital Broadcasting Systems for Television; Implementation Guidelines for the Use of MPEG-2 Systems; Video and Audio in Satellite and Cable Broadcasting Applications," November 1994.

7. ITU-R Document, 10-11S/TEMP/26, "Digital Multi-programme Television Broadcast by Satellite," 28 November 1994.

8. ITU-R Document 11/BL/81, "Enhanced Compatible Widescreen Television Based on Conventional Television Systems," 21 March 1994.

9. SMPTE S17.391, SMPTE Draft Standard, "For Television, Bit-Serial Digital Interface for Interlaced 483-Active Line Scanning Systems," August 1994.

10. SMPTE S17.394, SMPTE Draft Standard, "For Television, Bit-Serial Digital Interface for Progressive 483-Active Line Scanning Systems," August 1994.

11. SMPTE S17.393, SMPTE Draft Standard, "For Television, Bit-Serial Digital Interface for Progressive 720-Active Line Scanning Systems," August 1994.

12. ITU-R Document 11/19, Draft Revision of Recommendation ITU-R BT.1117, "Studio Format Parameters for Enhanced 16:9 625-line Television Systems (D- and D2-MAC, PAL-plus, Enhanced SECAM), 28 October 1994.

13. ITU-R Document 11A/TEMP/1, "Terms for Three-Dimensional/Stereoscopic Television," 13 October 1994.

14. CCIR Document 11/22, "Design of a System of Stereoscopic Television," 21 May 1958.

15. CCIR Document 11/744, 28 November 1989, p. 3.

16. CCIR Report 312-5, "Constitution of a System of Stereoscopic Television," 1990.

17. Document 11/585, "Experimental Stereoscopic Television System Utilizing HDTV Equipment," Japan, 1989.

18. ITU-R Document 11A/TEMP/11, "Stereoscopic Television Based on R- and L-Eye Two Channel Signals," 18 October 1994.

19. ITU-R Document 11D/TEMP/14, "Service and Programme Information Data for Digital Broadcasting Systems," 18 October 1994.

9

Interactive Television Broadcasting

As societies are becoming more mobile, both in personal and work-related activities, people are moving more often, traveling more readily, and spending more time outside the office. In this environment, interactive systems need to evolve from dependence on fixed communications systems that require people to be in specific locations to interactive services that, in themselves, provide mobility.[1]

Interactive communications services allow viewers to select and modify programming choices, presentation, and content by providing a return path from the receiver to the source upon which viewers can signal their preferences. Mechanisms for providing a return path over telephone, cable links, public land-mobile telecommunications systems, or even radio-frequency links from the home are easily as envisioned as is a telephone conversation: a basic form of interactive communications.

In 1994, the ITU Radiocommunications Assembly recognized that the rapid progress toward digital television delivery services using terrestrial, cable, and satellite broadcasting communications would be enhanced if mechanisms were provided for use in receiving information related to the program material from viewers. Such mechanisms offer the possibility of viewer interacting with the program vision, sound, and data services. In 1994, the ITU drafted a question and established a Rapporteur Group to study possible return-path mechanisms.[2]

INTRODUCTION

The ITU has defined interactive services as services in which the end-user influences in real-time or quasi-real-time the content of the services delivered by sending messages to the service origination point.[3] This definition does not cover services where the user interacts locally with data that are down-loaded, although this type of service may provide a basic level of interactivity. Full interactive broadcast communications are two-way communications mechanisms that are not physically attached to a cable or telephone wire.

The ITU efforts to develop interactive communications standards were launched with the adoption of a draft new Question (Document 11/216) on "Interactive Television Broadcasting Systems." The Question considers:

> the progress in information processing and transmission technologies; the rapid progress towards enhanced and digital television delivery systems using terrestrial, cable, satellite, and network channels; the need for such systems for interactivity for a variety of purposes; the development of transmission methods suitable for use in receiving from viewers information related to the vision, sound, and data program material; and the large number of domestic receivers likely to be impacted by the adoption of interactive services.

This requires the development of an understanding of existing and proposed interactive services and consideration of the varied applications that are under development, leading to a standard method or protocol for a return channel.[4] The list of principle tasks can be summarized as follows:

1. To describe the various types of interactive services that are likely to be implemented and the requirements they place on a return channel
2. To determine the location of possible return-path channels from the receiver to the broadcaster and/or other users of such data for different reception media and the appropriate transmission, modulation, and management techniques to be implemented for such channels
3. To determine return methods (protocols) for the various services.

The second point focuses on the issues of frequency allocation and planning factors and service objectives that are best suited for such systems, seeking to identify the possibilities for harmonious use of other data communications channels such as switched network or personal communications service systems that can provide an appropriate return channel for interactive broadcasting.

Broadcast interactive services have the potential to provide significant benefits to the user but will require solving complex technological and public policy questions. The primary challenges to the introduction of a broadcast interactive service involve the appropriate use of the spectrum, the ability to provide ubiquitous coverage, and developing an effective user "appliance."

It would seem that incorporating an interactive capability into the television receiver, as the "appliance" by which most consumers will interface to the global information infrastructure, is a natural step in the evolution of communications services. The anticipated growth of such services implies a need to accommodate thousands of narrowband digital channels. Further, the use of modern cellular digital communication technologies, public land–mobile telecommunications systems (FPLMTS), low earth orbit satellite (LEOS) links, and other technologies to implement the return path indicates that a common technical approach is highly possible.

In March 1995, on the basis of preliminary studies by the Study Group 11 Special Rapporteur, an ITU/ UNESCO pilot project on interactive television systems for distance learning applications was elaborated by the ITU and UNESCO. The use of interactive television in this context opens the door to a new strategy of mass telecommunication services and positions the television appliance as an intellectual device. The digital television appliance, equipped with complex signal processors to accomplish the task of decoding the digital data stream that carries the television service, forms the basis of a new class of consumer appliances termed a "teleputer."[5]

The primary goal is the development of an effective broadcast interactive system that utilizes existing broadcasting bands, over cable, telephone lines, or satellite. Establishing a worldwide standard provides economies of scale, new market opportunities, and standardization of equipment for use throughout the world.[6]

Interactive video systems, thus, become of interest to developing countries and educational institutions. The television receiver, as the most ubiquitous communications appliance, will allow communication both to and from the viewer. The television appliance can be connected by way of the return channels to information centers. Program and other content providers will be challenged to provide program content for the interactive environment. A broadcast communications interactive capability unlocks the levels of personal freedom and control over communications that match society's growing mobility.

System Issues

Possible system implementation scenarios involve use of spectrum to accommodate return channels within alternative media such as telephone systems, cable systems, and broadcast satellite channels and include assignment of portions of existing terrestrial services to a return channel. In each case, the fundamental issues are avoidance of overcrowding of the radio-frequency spectrum and protection against increased interference characteristics that might diminish the quality of existing services. Possible solutions might be found in the use of multiplexing technologies such as time-division multiple access (TDMA) and code-division multiple access (CDMA). TDMA employs compression technologies and multiplexing of bit streams to enable multiple transmissions on the same frequency. CDMA is based on spread-spectrum technologies.

Providing ubiquitous coverage does not necessarily imply using a single ubiquitous implementation, although a universal mechanism is highly desirable. System implementation must take into consideration that system usage will not be evenly distributed throughout the globe. Approximately 75% of the surface of the earth is covered by water, population densities are not geographically uniform due to local variations in the earth's ability to support populations, and variations in local economic conditions will lead to variations in demands for service.

Possible solutions abound. The ideal solution would be agreement on a single band to be designated for interactive services. This would create a global market providing benefits of scale in recovery of equipment design and manufacture costs and increased market competition. Other spectrum possibilities include the use of excess capacity in low earth orbit service satellite facilities and use of a personal communications systems (PCS) service infrastructure. Initial studies by the ITU noted that the bandwidth of the return channel will depend not only on the data rate of the service but also on the specific choice of the frequency band, particularly where that band may be shared with other services.[7] The level of demand, the condition of the local communications infrastructure, and variations in local propagation characteristics will influence the choice of technology implemented in a particular region of the world.

INTERACTIVE SERVICES

Digital television systems using packetized data streams and packet headers allow the service provider to consider offering a diverse program content. Diversity of programming in a service that allows multiple programs to reside in a single service channel implies the possibility of multimedia services.[8] An understanding of the types of services that might be envisioned is necessary to determine systems requirements. A number of advanced data broadcasting service applications have been identified and are summarized in Tables 9-1 through 9-3. The characteristics of these services may be defined by a series of parameters which describe the service demands in terms of bit rate, return-path requirements, and local resource requirements.

Table 9-1. Mainstream Program-Related Services.

Service	Description	Comp.[a]	Rate[b]	Path[c]
Program guide or service information (SI)	Description of programs available from content provider. Guides may be customized to viewers' preferences.	V, A, T, I, G, D	k	N
Subtitling	Subtitles to be overlaid in the image at receiving end. Different services in different languages are possible.	T, I, G	k	N
Summary	A summary of the program, updated during the course of the program.	V, A, T, I, G, D	k	N
Program description	A description of the ongoing program for benefit of hearing-impaired or visually-impaired viewers.	A, T, D	k	N
Home shopping	Interaction from the viewer to make inquiries or to place an order.	V, A, T, I	k	Y-k
Audience polling	Viewers answer polling questions. Viewers choose outcome of program.	V, A, D	b	Y-b
Auctioning/gambling	Placing of bids, bets, etc.	V, A, T, I, G, D	k	Y-b
Multiprogram choice	Selection of one program from a multichannel package, such as camera position in a sport program, additional data in a news program, etc., or for near-video on demand.	V, A, T, I, G, D	M	b[d]
Extra information	Viewer control of additional information or services related to program.	A, T, D	k	N

Notes: a: Service components: V = video; A = audio; T = text; I = images (stills); G = graphics; D = data (control data, coded data, etc.).

b: Assumed data rate in bits/s (i.e., k = kbits/s, M = Mbits/s, etc.).

c: Return path required (N = No, Y-r = Yes) with assumed data rate.

d: A transmission rate of a few 100 bits/s is considered sufficient to control a virtual video recorder.

Table 9-2. Down-Loaded Information.

Service	Description	Comp.[a]	Rate[b]	Path[c]
Program guide or service information (SI)	Description of programs available from content provider. Guides may be customized to viewers' preferences.	V, A, T, I, G, D	k	N
Subtitling	Subtitles to be overlaid in the image at receiving end. Different services in different languages are possible.	T, I, G	k	N
Resumé	A summary of the program, updated during the course of the program.	V, A, T, I, G, D	k	N
Program description	A description of the ongoing program for benefit of hearing-impaired or visually-impaired viewers.	A, T, D	k	N
Home shopping	Interaction from the viewer to make inquiries or to place an order.	V, A, T, I	k	Y-k
Audience polling	Viewers answer polling questions. Viewers choose outcome of program.	V, A, D	b	Y-b
Auctioning/gambling	Placing of bids, bets, etc.	V, A, T, I, G, D	k	Y-b
Multiprogram choice	Selection of one program from a multichannel package, such as camera position in a sport program, additional data in a news program, etc., or for near-video on demand.	V, A, T, I, G, D	M	N
Extra information	Viewer control of additional information or services related to program.	A, T, D	k	N

Notes: a: Service components: V = video; A = audio; T = text; I = images (stills); G = graphics; D = data (control data, coded data, etc.).

b: Assumed data rate in bits/s (i.e., k = kbits/s, M = Mbits/s, etc.).

c: Return path required (N = No, Y-r = Yes) with assumed data rate.

Table 9-3. Appliance (Device) Dependent Services.

Service	Description	Comp.[a]	Rate[b]	Path[c]
Computer games	Down-loaded games to devices with appropriate processing power. Also two or more player environments with appropriate communications	D	M	Y-b
Database storage	Information storage (audio, photo, CD-interactive, CD-ROM, etc.) with local recording capability.	D	b–M	Y–b
Software	Down-loaded upgrades of operating systems, computer programs, program-related software for interactive services.	D	k	Y–b
Addressed data	Information addressed to a specific appliance or peripheral device.	V, A, T, I, G, D	b–M	Y–b

Notes: a: Service components: V = video; A = audio; T = text; I = images (stills); G = graphics; D = data (control data, coded data, etc.).

b: Assumed data rate in bits/s (i.e., k = kbits/s, M = Mbits/s, etc.).

c: Return path required (N = No, Y-r = Yes) with assumed data rate. For most of these services the return channel provides the mechanism to purchase license to use.

MECHANISMS FOR RETURN CHANNELS

Interactive services require a mechanism for the viewer to directly affect or respond to the program service being watched. The mechanism is a real-time communication channel from the consumer to the program source. This channel is called a "return path," a "return channel," or a "back channel." The simplest form of return channel is a telephone message back to the service provider such as occurs during audience polling when the viewers are asked to call one of several numbers to register their views (votes). The digital receiver could be constructed with a modem and phone connection allowing the consumer to use the remote device or a keyboard to construct the message to the program source. The digital receiver could then initiate the call, transfer the required data, establish a confirmation, and disconnect.

Cable Return Channels

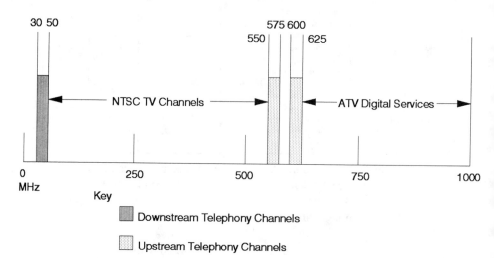

Figure 9-1. Cable System Frequency Allocation.

Cable systems provide a wide-band service capability (1000 MHz) and the ability to reconfigure the use of the spectrum as new services and technologies are introduced. Various proposals for placement of the return channels within a cable system utilize the 5–30 MHz spectrum and/or spectrum carved out of the high end of the band above 550 MHz as shown in Figure 9-1. Figure 9-1 shows a typical frequency allocation plan for a 1000-MHz cable system. Below 550 MHz, the system is identical to existing systems supporting analog television services in the 50–550 MHz band with a return path supported in a 5–30 MHz band. Return channels on copper wire in the 5–30 MHz range suffer from interference from amateur radio, CB-type transmitters, and other sources; systems in this range may require forward error correction or other protection means to achieve desirable error rates. Further, the 5–30 MHz spectrum may not contain sufficient bandwidth to service a truly universal interactive service environment. The use of optical fiber will reduce some of the interference issues, although the wiring between the cable set-top decoder, the VCR, and the television receiver may act as an antenna, collecting undesirable signals from the environment and introducing them into the return channel.

If (as shown in Figure 9-1) 25-MHz bandwidth return paths are provided for in the system, then 24 T1 channels could be supported. Because each T1 channel supports 24 voice channels, 576 voice circuits could be available in a 25-MHz-wide return path.[9]

One approach based on trunking proposes to support between 500 and 1000 subscribers with telephony services in a single 6-MHz television channel. The trunking approach provides each subscriber with on-demand access to a group of shared traffic channels. When a return-path request is initiated by a subscriber, the system assigns one of the available traffic channels to that subscriber for the duration of the message transfer. After completion, the assigned traffic channel is returned to the common pool for reassignment. Given that many return-path messages may be in the range of a few kbits, such a system could support a multitude of viewers.[10]

Cellular Communications

Digital, packet-switched data services are provided by the standard, cellular digital packet data (CDPD) network, utilizing the analog cellular telephone infrastructure. CDPD was developed as a mechanism for high-speed wireless data transmission to subscribers. This approach would use the same components found in the existing tens of millions of cellular telephones for the interactive appliance transmission device and affords the possibility of using standard network protocols such as TCP/IP and authentication and encryption technology.[11]

Satellite Systems

The ITU Rapporteur Group on Interactive Television Broadcasting identified several possible satellite systems with potential excess capacity for interactive services. Motorola's Iridium project is aimed at narrowband mobile services at rates as much as 2400 bits/s. A 73-satellite network, Iridium, by the terms of its FCC license, is a mobile service aimed at hand-held appliances. Teledesic plans to have a network of 840 low-orbit satellites offering a broad array of interactive voice, data, and video services. The Teledesic system promises transmission in the Mbits/s range.[12]

Interactive Protocols

In order for an interactive system to function properly, the program source must be able to identify the address of the end-user who is interacting with the system, so that proper services can be provided. Therefore, regardless of the technology used for providing a return channel, a handshaking protocol must be established. The world community would be best served by an agreement on a single protocol. The modulation and coding used will depend on the return channel system characteristics, but a common protocol can be established in which each message is contained in packets with headers that provide identification of the end-user and, where necessary, verification of payment for services.

END NOTES

1. Document 11F/5, "Study Group 11 Rapporteur Group on Interactive Television Broadcasting Systems—Preliminary Report," 15 June 1994.

2. Draft New Question [ITU-R Doc. 11/216, Rev. 2], "Interactive Broadcasting Systems."

3. ITU-R Document 11-3/74, "Terminology for New Services and Technologies Adopted by ITU-T Study Group 9," 18 November 1994.

4. A return channel is a communications channel established between the end-user and the service origination point that allows the user to interact with the service origination.

5. ITU Document 11/79, "Report of the Chairman of Study Group 11," 17 May 1995, p. 32.

6. ITU Document 11F/5, "Study Group 11 Rapporteur Group on Interactive Television Broadcasting Systems—Preliminary Report," 15 June 1994.

7. ITU Document 11C/TEMP/12, "Draft Liaison Statement to Working Party 8A," 18 October 1994.

8. Multimedia services are services in which the interchanged information consists of more than one type and may include text, graphics, sound, images, and video.

9. One T1 channel = 1.544 Mbits/s. A QPSK modulation scheme = 2 b/Hz, implying that a T1 channel requires 0.722 MHz of bandwidth. Adding a 30% channel guard band implies that a T1 channel requires 1 MHz of bandwidth. Therefore, a 25-MHz return path could support 24 T1 services with appropriate guard bands.

10. ITU Document Rapporteur Group on Interactive Television Broadcasting Systems/TEMP/6, "Delivery of Interactive Television Services over the Existing Fiber/Coax Infrastructure," 8 September 1994.

11. ITU Document Rapporteur Group on Interactive Television Broadcasting Systems/TEMP/11, "Wireless Data Transmission," 8 September 1994.

12. ITU Document Rapporteur Group on Interactive Broadcasting Systems/TEMP/7, "Satellite Systems with Possible Excess Capacity for Interactive Services," 8 September 1994.

10

Quality Assessment and Measurement Technology

Determining the appropriate technology to be applied to a television service requires that there be a reliable and consistent mechanism to evaluate and compare the technologies under investigation. Quality assessment and measurement techniques have been developed by the ITU-R that provide mechanisms for describing the quality of image and sound services. Quality assessment mechanisms can be used for the process of both system and parameter selection. Subjective assessment measurement methods are useful in establishing the reactions of the users of the services. When subjective assessments are used to establish the performance of the services under optimum conditions, they are called "quality assessments." When subjective assessments are used to establish the performance of the services under nonoptimum conditions such as found in transmission media, they are called "impairment assessments." Objective measurements are those which measure service technical performance under specified operating conditions. The work of the ITU recognizes that characterization of service performance by objective means may not always be possible, and when required, objective methods may be supplemented by subjective measurements.

INTRODUCTION

Both images and sound are inherently analog systems. The process of capturing a scene and transmitting it to the human brain requires illumination of the scene and presenting the reflection of that illumination with its infinite variation of light and color intensity to the eye. Imaging is essentially an analog light-to-light process even if some of the interim steps are processed in the digital domain. Sound is also an inherently analog process; vibrations generated at a source at various amplitudes and frequencies are transmitted to the human hearing system for recognition as analog signals regardless of whether digital processing occurs in the process.

QUALITY ASSESSMENT

Conducting appropriate subjective assessments requires establishing a set of conditions that best meet the objectives and conditions under which the assessment must operate. This means establishing the following:

- A set of viewing conditions
- Selecting appropriate test material
- Selection of appropriate test methods
- Agreeing on a grading method.

The ITU has developed a set of general viewing conditions as described in Table 10-1.

The viewing distance, maximum observation angle, and the peak luminance of the screen should be determined on the basis of the application being addressed. Viewing distance may be of two types. A viewing distance may be selected based on the characteristics of the system and may be based on the viewing distance being a specified multiple of the display picture height as a function of the resolution of the system. The viewing

distance for evaluation of conventional television systems is generally set at six times the display picture
height, whereas the viewing distance for evaluation of
high-definition television (HDTV) systems is generally
set at three times the display picture height. Alternatively, as with home viewing, the viewing distance may
be based on a "preferred viewing distance" determined
by the measurements of some assumed "average home
viewing room" and furniture placement.

Table 10-1. General Viewing Conditions.[1]

Parameter	Value
Luminance of inactive screen to peak luminance ratio	0.02
Screen black level luminance to peak luminance ratio	0.01
Display brightness and contrast setup	PLUGE
Maximum observation angle relative to the normal	30
Luminance of background behind picture display to peak luminance ratio	0.15
Chromaticity of background	D_{65}
Other room illumination	Low

The test materials selected should also reflect the set of
assessment problems that are under study. Table 10-2
provides a list of assessment problems and types of test
materials that address these problems.

Test materials could (and should) reflect the range of
image sequences that might appear over the service in
question. For instance, the testing of standards conversion between 525-line and 625-line systems might
include material such as sporting events with background detail (crowds in an audience) and high motion
in the foreground to test the vertical-temporal characteristics of the conversion process. In general, critical
material is included in order to provide a basis for inter-
preting the results, where noncritical material would

provide no baseline for such interpretation. The phrase "critical but not unduly so" implies that the pictures fall within the range of image sequences that might appear on the service. The source signals should be of optimum quality for the system under investigation.

Table 10-2. Assessment Test Material.[2]

Assessment Problem	Material Used
Overall performance with average material	General, "critical but not unduly so"
Capacity, critical applications (e.g., contribution, post-production, etc.)	A range, including very critical material for the application tested
Performance of "adaptive" systems	Material very critical for "adaptive" scheme used
Identify weaknesses and possible improvements	Critical, attribute-specific material
Identify factors on which systems seem to vary	Wide range of very rich material
Conversion among different standards	Critical for differences (e.g., field rate)

Table 10-3 provides a list of particular assessment problems and methods used to assess them.

The ITU process, as described in ITU-R BT.500, suggests that at least 15 observers be used, that a screening and training program be provided to sensitize the observers to a set of attributes under study, and that test sessions last up to half an hour.

During the testing, observers are asked to grade an image or image sequence according to a set of scales. The grading may reflect judgments on whether or not a specific attribute or set of attributes is detected. Such attributes may establish the impairment threshold. Scales that assess image quality or image impairments are most often used, and the ITU-R Recommendation BT.500 scale is shown in Table 10-4. In some cases of operational monitoring, half-grades are used, and other scales have been developed to allow assessment of special attributes. Table 10-5 provides a sample scale for evaluating graphics in teletext and similar services.

Table 10-3. Assessment Test Methods.[3]

Assessment Problem	Method Used
Measure the quality of systems relative to a reference.	Double stimulus continuous-quality method (Rec. ITU-R BT.500-5, s5)
Measure the robustness (failure characteristics) of systems.	Double stimulus impairment method (Rec. ITU-R BT.500-5, s4)
Quantify the quality of systems when no reference is available.	Ratio-scaling method or categorical scaling (Report ITU-R BT.1082-1)
Compare the quality of alternative systems when no reference is available.	Ratio-scaling method or categorical scaling (Report ITU-R BT.1082-1)
Identify factors on which systems are perceived to differ and measure the perceptual influence.	Method under study (Report ITU-R BT.1082-1)
Establish the point at which an impairment becomes visible.	Threshold estimation by forced-choice method or method of adjustment (Report ITU-R BT.1082-1)
Determine whether systems are perceived to differ.	Force-choice method (Report ITU-R BT.1082-1)

Table 10-4. ITU-R Quality and Impairment Scale; Five-Grade Scale.[4]

Quality Level	Impairment
5 Excellent	5 Imperceptible
4 Good	4 Perceptible, but not annoying
3 Fair	3 Slightly annoying
2 Poor	2 Annoying
1 Bad	1 Very annoying

Table 10-5. Legibility and Reading Effort Scale.[5]

Quality of Legibility	Reading Effort Scale
Excellent legibility	No reading effort
Good legibility	Attention necessary, but no appreciable reading effort
Fair legibility	Moderate reading effort
Poor legibility	Substantial reading effort
Bad legibility	Very substantial reading effort

The subjective assessment of digital systems requires methodologies that take into consideration the picture and sound content failure characteristics, the probability of occurrence, and the quality goals of the service. The subjective assessment of digital systems requires digital-specific measurement criteria and tools, the statistical processing of an adequate number of image and sound files, and the development of optimized algorithms for processing.

MEASUREMENT TECHNOLOGY

Introduction

The measurement of digital video and audio equipment must take into consideration the characteristics of and impairments to the analog signal caused by the digital process. ITU-R Study Group 11 has developed a set of Recommendations and test signals that are intended to assist in measuring the analog characteristics such as the signal-to-noise ratio (SNR), differential gain and phase (dG, dP), and the nonlinearity of the equipment, as well as the variations in the results of those measurements caused by quantization errors in the coding process. One of the techniques used is the addition of a dithering signal to the signal being measured to stabilize measured values by causing very small random changes to the level of the test signals and, thereby, dispersing the quantization errors evenly in relation to the quantization levels.[6] Study Group 11 has also developed a series of Recommended test signals such as color bars[7] and color ramps.[8]

Digital Coding Considerations

As noted in the previous chapters, the function of digital coding of images is to reduce the bit rate required to represent the image sequences while minimizing loss of quality and impairments to the images. Some of the impairments can be objectively measured and the measurements can be related to some quantification of codec quality based on comparative data related to the interpretation of observers developed through subjective testing. A list of quality impairment factors is given in Table 10-6.

Table 10-6. Examples of Picture-Impairment Factors.[9]

Picture-Impairment Factor	Physical Measure
Image blur	Step response rise time
Edge busyness	Step response jitter width
False contouring	S_{p-p} to minimum quantizing p-p
Granular noise	Equivalent analog signal SNR expressed as S_{p-p}/N_{rms}
"Dirty window"	Maximum noise amplitude
Movement blur	Rise time of a moving edge
Jerkiness	Field or frame difference in terms of moving edge position

Natural image sequences are image sequences that might normally be found in the service being provided. Natural picture sequences can be used as a means of evaluating image impairments. They can be thought of as being composed of a number of different areas, each area having a different content and exercising a different aspect of the digital codec. Where two different codecs are being compared, the image sequence can be used to determine which appears better. Sequences that might be chosen for subjective assessment purposes should be evaluated for use as an objective measure of performance. Synthetic test sequences can be also assembled that progressively take a codec to the point where visible distortion is produced.

The most common form of objective quality measurement of a codec is based on the coding error, which is the difference between the image sequence input of the codec and the decoded output. The difference signal can be displayed as an image sequence and provide useful information. An often used measure of decoded image quality is the mean square coding error. This value is the average over every picture sample in the sequence of the square of the coding error, usually normalized with respect to the square of the full amplitude of the image samples. This normalized mean square error N is quoted as a coding noise figure of $-10 \log N$. Because it is an average value, this measure does not distinguish between a few large coding errors that could be annoying to the observer and a large number of imperceptible, small coding errors.

The ITU-R suggests that the performance of a particular codec be judged in two ways and under two sets of conditions. The first way is to judge performance using subjective assessment techniques. The second way is to judge performance using objective measurement techniques. The two sets of conditions should include evaluation under optimum performance conditions, which tends to form a baseline and evaluation under progressively noisier conditions that help to determine the threshold of usability.

The ITU-R suggests[10] that although it is both possible and valid to assess digital codec using still images, the use of moving image sequences allows both a more realistic representation of television services and easier observation of noise processes. The sequences should exercise codec response to static and moving textured areas (both luminance and chrominance texture), static and moving objects with high contrast edges with various orientation (both luminance and chrominance edges), static plain mid-gray areas, just-perceptible source noise, live complex camera sequences, and synthetic (computer-generated) sequences (free from camera imperfections such as scanning aperture and lag). Examples of complex camera motion are scenes employing simultaneous zoom and panning of the camera, scenes with textured backgrounds with perhaps detailed objects accelerating in the foreground, and scenes with rotating three-dimensional objects. Synthetically generated sequences should be both simple and complex. Sequences should be at least 10 s in duration, but preferably 15–30 s.

Evaluation of system performance under varying coding levels and transmission noise environment can be obtained by measurement of a minimum of five bit-error ratios or selected transmission conditions spaced so that the range of samples gives rise to system impairments from "imperceptible" to "very annoying."

Statistical Methods

Work performed by the Broadcasting Technology Association of Japan[11] (BTA) in support of the ITU effort uses statistical measurements as a means of determining digital system performance. The BTA reported on the results of statistical measurements for a set of 60 standard moving sequences published by the Institute of Television Engineers of Japan (ITE).

The BTA selected the following statistic items from among the range of items which might serve to characterize the test materials:

1. AC energy of DCT (discrete cosine transform) coefficients
2. Spectral entropy of DCT coefficients
3. Motion vectors
4. Motion-compensated prediction error.

The BTA measurements were carried out only for luminance signals. Sample block sizes of 8 x 8 were applied for DCT calculations, whereas 16 x 8 sample blocks were applied for motion vector detection and motion compensation. Values were calculated for each block and averaged over a frame or field, as appropriate, to express the characteristics of that frame or field. Each of the ITE test sequences is of 15 s duration.

The AC energy value represents the degree of picture activity including picture fineness.[12] Four types of AC energy were calculated, as shown in Table 10-7.

Table 10-7. Four Types of AC Energy.

Type	Signal	DCT Block	Averaging
Field DCT	Normal	8 pixels x 8 lines in a field	In a field
Frame DCT	Normal	8 pixels x 8 lines in a frame	In a frame
Field DCT-FD	Frame difference	8 pixels x 8 lines in a field	In a field
Frame DCT-FD	Motion-compensated frame difference	8 pixels x 8 lines in a frame	In a frame

Spectral entropy represents the degree of randomness of the DCT coefficients and can be used to estimate the bit rate of the DCT-based bit-reduction system.[13] Motion vectors were calculated using the block-matching method in which the vector of the block is defined such that the sum of the absolute difference between the current frame and the previous frame displaced by the vector is a minimum value. The calculation was performed with simple precision (pel precision in the horizontal direction and two-line precision in the vertical direction).[14] The motion-compensated frame-difference signal represents the prediction error.[15] The power of the prediction error (EP) is defined to be the mean square value of the difference signal.[16] This latter statistical value can be used to estimate whether the sequence is critical for evaluating a bit-rate reduction system using motion compensation.

The mean value of the statistics over the 60 image sequences that are included in the ITE set are shown in Table 10-8.

Table 10-8. Mean Value Statistics over the ITE Sequences.

Statistic	Value Averaged over 60 Sequences
MC prediction-error power	– 30.4 dB
AC energy	
Field DCT	0.059
Frame DCT	0.052
Field DCT-FD	0.047
Frame DCT-MCFD	0.010
Spectral entropy	
Field DCT	2.5
Frame DCT	2.3
Field DCT-FD	2.1
Frame DCT-MCFD	1.5

Conventional Television Images

The ITU-R developed Recommendations on the criteria for the subjective assessment of digital television systems at or near the quality of conventional systems[17] and a set of associated test pictures and sequences[18] for use in performing the assessment. The specific viewing conditions established for use with conventional television systems are detailed in Table 10-9.

Table 10-9. Viewing Conditions for Conventional Television Subjective Assessment.

Item	Values
a Ratio of viewing distance to picture height	4H and 6H[a]
b Peak luminance on the screen (cd/m^2)	70
c Angle subtended by that part of the background which satisfies the specification above. This should be preserved for all observers.	> 43° H x 57° W
d Display size	> 56 cm (22 in.) (4:3) > 72 cm (28 in.) (16:9)[b]

Notes:

a. 6H is the preferred distance for the assessment of systems offering quality at or near that of conventional systems (525/60, 625/50). Using 4H also is acceptable, provided the results are stated separately.

b. ITU-R Document 11/BL/69, Draft Revision of Recommendation ITU-R BT.811, "The Subjective Assessment of Enhanced PAL and Secam Systems," 31 March 1994.

HDTV Images

Recognizing that the definition of principles and methods for measurement of an HDTV signal was an important part of the development of HDTV technology, a study program was proposed in 1989 on "Measurement in an HDTV Environment."[19] The proposed program included studies on methods for measuring the parameters of HDTV signals, methods for measuring and testing the performance of links or channels used for interconnecting equipment in a studio environment, and development of test signals and test patterns to be used in the assessment of performance of transmission channels.

The ITU has established Recommendations on test sequences for the subjective assessment of HDTV services.[20] The collection of sequences tests a multitude of

HDTV system attributes, although individual sequences may test only a few of these.

Technical measurements of HDTV were seen as important to their successful development. Advances in this area were also reflected in the output documents of the CCIR. These concerned both the subjective and objective measurements. Recommendation 710 on assessments defined the methods on determining picture quality. Testing centers were established in Moscow, Ottawa, and Washington, D.C., utilizing Recommendation 710 as the basis for evaluation.

The ability to indirectly access the subjective quality of television pictures in terms of objective television equipment had proven to be one of the more difficult challenges. Based on statistical processing of a large number of picture image files and on development of optimal algorithms for their processing, it was proposed that such television quality devices (**qualimeters**) can be designed. Such qualimeters constituted a new family of television measuring instruments. Exhaustive statistical data on HDTV quality obtained in Japan, in a number of European countries, and in the advanced television test centers in Moscow, Ottawa, and Washington, were seen as playing an important role in the development of HDTV qualimeters.

In 1988, Interim Working Party (IWP) 11/4, chaired by Mr. D. Wood (EBU), drew up a document which included recommended methods for subjective assessment of high-definition television. The work on subjective assessment was firmly based on CCIR Recommendation 500, which outlined a number of preferred subjective assessment methods for conventional systems (525/60 and 625/50). This work recognized that many of the methodological details described in Recommendation 500 were also appropriate within the context of HDTV. The primary differences between conventional system and HDTV approaches to subjective assessment lie in the viewing conditions. The recommendation on viewing conditions as they apply to HDTV are found in Table 10-10. The study of this work continues in Working Party 11-E, chaired by Mr. J. Tejerina (Spain).

Table 10-10. Viewing Conditions for HDTV Subjective Assessment.[21]

Item		Values[a]
a	Ratio of viewing distance to picture height	3
b	Peak luminance on the screen (cd/m^2)[b]	150–250
c	Ratio of luminance of inactive tube screen (beam cuts off) to peak luminance[c]	≤ 0.02
d	Ratio of the luminance of the screen when displaying only black level in a completely dark room to that corresponding to peak white[d]	Approximately 0.01
e	Ratio of luminance of background behind picture monitor to peak luminance of picture	Approximately 0.02
f	Illumination from other sources[e]	Low
g	Chromaticity of background	D_{65}
h	Angle subtended by that part of the background which satisfies the specification above.[f] This should be preserved for all observers.	53° H x 83° W
i	Arrangement of observers	Within ± 30° horizontally from the center of the display. The vertical limit is under study.
j	Display size[g]	1.4 m (55 in.)

Notes:

a. Values for b and j are as specified in Report 1216. As it may not be currently possible to achieve these conditions fully for tests, alternative values are given on an interim basis. It should be recognized, however, that the results of tests conducted under the interim conditions may not be, in general, comparable with those obtained in situations in which Report 1216 presentation objectives apply.

b. Peak luminance on the screen corresponding to the video signal with 100% amplitude. Values > 70 cd/m² should be used until the specified level becomes technically feasible.

c. This item could be influenced by the room illumination as well as the contrast range of the display.

d. Black level corresponds to the video signal with 0% amplitude.

e. Room illumination should be set in order to make it possible to satisfy conditions c and e.

f. A minimum of 28° high by 48° wide is recommended.

g. Values ≥ 76.2 cm (30 in.) should be used if displays of the specified size are not available.

It was observed that the establishment of monitoring techniques and appropriate devices must precede HDTV system implementation so that by the time such systems were brought into service, a usable measurement database would be available. The range of usable techniques was seen as wide, ranging from the insertion of known special test frames into the television signal and analysis of the received image, to monitoring the constellations of the modulated carrier(s), to bit-error rate (BER) measurement on the demodulated and decoded data stream at both the transmitter and receiver locations, to monitoring error tokens in the received data stream. By applying these techniques, the quality of the decoded images could be optimized. Automated systems used to monitor serviceability, system diagnostics, and predictive correction would be an essential part of the new digital service. The speed of corrective action could be increased by reducing the number of parameters that must be monitored. This could be accomplished by establishing correlations among them, identifying the representative characteristics, and specifying integrated assessment criteria for picture quality and channel performance assessments. The results of such monitoring could then be used for automatic adjustment and correction.

Multiprogram Services

The ITU-R recognized that a variety of media (e.g., terrestrial transmission, satellite, and cable) with different transmission characteristics may be used for the delivery of multiprogram services and, further, that there is a relationship between the number of channels in a multiprogram multiplex and the perceived quality of those services. The service quality delivered by any individual program service will vary according to either the scene content of the program service or the content of other program services in the multiplex where statistical methods are used to alter the data space assigned to any one program on a dynamic basis.[22]

EVOLUTION OF MEASUREMENT TECHNOLOGY

David Wood (EBU) noted[23] that as imaging and sound systems evolve, they will bring new challenges to the science of system quality evaluation. A firmly grounded and well-documented methodology for evaluating new systems is necessary to selection of desirable system parameters. A radical change in the approach to measuring existing 6-, 7-, and 8-MHz channels is seen as necessary to accommodate the planned transmission of signals for advanced television systems, including enhanced television, HDTV, and multiprogram signals. Such systems would contain either a hybrid analog–digital picture signal or a fully digital picture signal supported by digital sound and data signals, test signals, and other system control and data signals. Therefore, new measuring signals and methods for processing them in the existing channels are required in consideration of the wide variety of information transmitted. The ITU-R has developed the methodology for making the necessary measurements.

END NOTES

1. ITU-R Document 11/BL/66, Draft Revision of Recommendation ITU-R BT.500-5, "Methodology for the Subjective Assessment of the Quality of Television Pictures," 31 March 1994, p. 3.

2. ITU-R Document 11/BL/66, "Methodology for the Subjective Assessment of the Quality of Television Pictures," 31 March 1994, p. 5.

3. ITU-R Document 11/BL/66, "Methodology for the Subjective Assessment of the Quality of Television Pictures," 31 March 1994, p. 7.

4. ITU-R Document 11/BL/66, "Methodology for the Subjective Assessment of the Quality of Television Pictures," 31 March 1994, p. 14.

5. ITU-R BT. Recommendation 812, "Subjective Assessment of the Quality of Alphanumeric and Graphic Pictures in Teletext and Similar Services," 1992.

6. ITU-R Document 11B/TEMP/9, Draft New Recommendation, "Measuring Methods for Digital Video Equipment with Analog Input/Output," 17 October 1994.

7. ITU-R BT.471 Recommendation, "Nomenclature and Description of Colour Bar Signals," 1970–1986.

8. ITU-R BT.801 Recommendation, "Test Signals for Digitally Encoded Colour Television Signals Conforming with Recommendations 601 and 656," 1992.

9. ITU-R Recommendation 813, "Methods for Objective Picture Quality Assessment in Relation to Impairments from Digital Coding of Television Signals," 1992.

10. ITU-R Document 11/BL/67, Draft New Recommendation ITU-R BT. [Doc. 11/182], "Subjective Assessment of Digital Television Systems at or Near the Quality of Conventional Systems," 31 March 1994.

11. ITU-R Document 11E/15, "Statistics of Test Sequences for HDTV Subjective Measurement," 5 October 1994.

12. AC energy is defined as the square sum of the DCT coefficients without the DC (0, 0) coefficient:

$$AC = (1/N) \, ac_k \, / \, AC_{max},$$

$$ac_k = \; C(m, n)^2 - C(0, 0)^2,$$

where $C(m, n)$ denotes the DCT coefficients,

N is the number of blocks in a field or frame, and

AC_{max} is the normalizing factor, a theoretical maximum value obtained when half the area within a block is white and half the area within the block is black.

13. Spectral entropy is represented by the equation

$$SE = \; (1/N)(se_k)^2,$$

where: $se_k = \; C(m, n) \, / A \log_2 [C(m, n) \, / A]$, and $A = C(m, n)$.

14. Two types of statistics were used to express the degree of motion of the picture, mean magnitude of the vectors averaged over a field, and standard deviation within the field. Separate calculations were performed for the horizontal and vertical directions:

$$u_X = (1/M) \, X_k \; \text{and} \; u_Y = \; (1/M) \, Y_k,$$

$$s_{X2} = \; (1/M) \, X_{k2} - u_{X2} \; \text{and} \; s_{Y2} = (1/M) \, Y_{k2} - u_{Y2},$$

where X_k and Y_k denote the horizontal and vertical components of the vector in the block, respectively,

u_X and u_Y denote the mean magnitude of X_k and Y_k averaged over a field, respectively,

s_X and s_Y denote the standard deviation of X_k and Y_k, respectively, and

M denotes the number of blocks in a field.

15. The motion-compensated frame-difference signal is expressed

$$e_k (x, y) = f_0 (x, y) - f_1 (x - u_k, y - v_k)$$

where $e_k(*)$, $f_0(*)$, and $f_1(*k)$ denote the motion-compensated frame-difference signal in the kth block, the current frame signal, and the previous frame signal, respectively, whereas u_k, v_k denote the horizontal and vertical components of the motion vector in the block, respectively.

16. $EP = (1/M) \ ep_k$,

where $ep_k = [1/(16 \times 8)] \ e(x, y)^2$.

17. ITU-R Document 11/BL/67, Draft New Recommendation ITU-R BT. [Doc. 11/182], "Subjective Assessment of Digital Television Systems at or Near the Quality of Conventional Systems," 31 March 1994.

18. ITU-R Document 11/BL/68, Draft Revision of Recommendation ITU-R BT.802, "Test Pictures and Sequences for Subjective Assessment of Digital Codecs Conveying Signals Produced According to Recommendation ITU-R BT.601," 31 March 1994.

19. CCIR Document 11/361-E, "Proposal for a New Study Programme, Measurement in an HDTV Environment, U.S.S.R.," 11 May 1989.

20. ITU-R BT.710, "Subjective Assessment Methods for Image Quality in High-Definition Television," Annex 4.

21. CCIR Recommendation 710, "Subjective Assessment Methods for Image Quality in High-Definition Television," 1990.

22. ITU Document 11E/TEMP/10, Draft New Recommendation, "Assessment of the Quality of Multi-Programme Services," 19 October 1994.

23. "ITU Handbook on Subjective Assessment Methodology," 1994, p. 1.

11

Harmonization and Interoperability

The ITU-R considers all aspects of the broadcast chain from production through reception. The members of the international community participating in the work of ITU-R recognized that the introduction of digital technology in imaging applications together with the widespread implementation of digital communications created an opportunity to establish a universal digital image and sound coding standard capable of meeting the needs of an unprecedented range of applications. The ITU-R set forth to define a universal service architecture and information infrastructure that was appropriate for use across a broad range of media and could serve as a means of harmonizing the needs of different industries and different regions of the world.

INTRODUCTION

The work in Study Group 11 on harmonizing digital imaging and sound services began in 1986 and was based on the development of a global approach to the issues under study considering the differing service requirements, the many possible communications applications that can be served by digital technology, and the necessity for harmonization between broadcasting and nonbroadcasting applications. The nonbroadcasting applications included the fields of film production, printing, medical applications, video conferencing, and high-resolution computer-imaging applications. Recognizing the need to provide interoperability between these additional applications, the chairman of Study Group 11 moved to the create an Interim Working Party (IWP) on harmonization.[1]

The work of harmonizing the differing requirements of the various interested industries and applications was assigned during the 1986–1990 study period to Interim Working Party (IWP) 11/9, chaired by Mr. R. Bedford (United Kingdom). IWP 11/9 was reorganized as a Task Group (TG11/4) at the beginning of the 1990–1994 study period and then as a permanent Working Party (11F) at the end of the 1990–1994 study period with Mr. Bedford continuing throughout as the chairman.

The work of Task Group 11/4 ranged from its first Recommendation on "Harmonization of digital methods for delivery systems for television services to the home" to establishing a Special Rapporteur on "Widescreen format implementation." One of the most important of the Task Group 11/4 reports was that of its ad hoc group on digital coding, chaired by Mr. T. Nishizawa (Japan), vice chairman of Study Group 11. This document contained a comprehensive description of the broadcasters' requirements and was forwarded as an input document to the ISO/IEC MPEG Group to assist this latter body in developing a standard that would meet broadcasters' needs.

The Task Group established a bridge between the Broadcasting Study Groups (SG10 and SG11) and the fast-moving ISO/MPEG project which proved to be beneficial to both groups and resulted in a set of widely accepted and useful new standards. Working Party 11F continued to investigate methods for improving the liaison, making it more timely and efficient, particularly in consideration of the working speed of the MPEG group, which required suitable input from the Study Groups with short response times.

Although Working Party 11F and its predecessor committees investigated a broad range of issues, the primary issues discussed in this chapter will deal with harmonization of DTTB services with conventional broadcasting services, satellite broadcasting, ATM (asynchronous transfer mode) switched data services, and interoperability at the receiver level.

HARMONIZING DTTB WITH CONVENTIONAL BROADCASTING SERVICES

The ITU-R has documented three nominal television bandwidth channels. The standard channel bandwidths are 6 MHz for Systems M and N (NTSC and PAL), 7 MHz for System B (PAL and SECAM), and 8 MHz for Systems G, H, I, D, K, K1, and L (SECAM and PAL).[2]

Terrestrial television broadcasting services are assigned to bands 8 (VHF) and 9 (UHF). In the VHF band, 6-MHz channels are the norm in 25 countries (13% of the total number of countries or geographical areas), 7-MHz channels are the norm in 68 countries (36%), and 8-MHz channels are the norm in 95 countries (51%). In the UHF band, 6-MHz channels are the norm in 14 countries (12%), 7-MHz channels are the norm in 6 countries (5%), and 8 MHz channels are the norm in 95 countries (83%). One of the goals of Task Group 11/3 was to determine the feasibility of establishing a single standards structure that would be appropriate for use in any of the standard channels. This concept was termed "HDTV-6-7-8."[3,4,5]

The HDTV-6-7-8 concept was based on the assumption that the difference among the bandwidths of the 6-,

7-, and 8-MHz channels could give rise to the development of three separate digital service scenarios each of which fully utilize the bandwidth of the assigned channels. It was assumed, however, that the 6-MHz implementation would have the potential to provide pictures of sufficiently high quality. The addition of a 1- or 2-MHz increment in the bandwidth could then be used to provide additional sound and data services because its use would not be critical for further improvement for domestic reception. On this basis, a proposal was put forth adopting a 6-MHz bandwidth core system for terrestrial television transmission networks and for cable television.

The application of digital signal-compression technology to coding conventional television signals allows accommodation of multiprogram transmission in the existing channels [multiprogram television (MPTV) 6-7-8 concept].[6,7] Compressed digital television systems offer the prospect of considerable improvement in service quality while appreciably improving spectrum utilization as compared with analog transmission methods. One way of exploiting these possibilities would be to use the bit stream available in digital terrestrial or satellite broadcasting to deliver a certain number of digitally compressed conventional television programs instead of a single conventional, enhanced- or high-definition program. These digitally compressed television signals would be accompanied by digital high-quality sound, coded conditional access information, and ancillary data channels. Furthermore, the same approach could be implemented in the transmission of multiprogram signals or stereoscopic television services over existing digital satellite or terrestrial links or cable television networks. The European digital video broadcasting (DVB) project paid particular attention to constructing a digital architecture that could accommodate both high-definition television (HDTV) and conventional television services and was interoperable over terrestrial broadcasting, cable, and satellite media. The DVB work led to a series of integrated European telecommunication standards covering digital broadcasting systems,[8] cable,[9] and satellite systems.[10,11] The DVB approach provides harmonization between services by using a unified, common method of video and audio source coding and a unified, common service multiplex and transport. This unified transport data stream is then provided with a framing structure, error protection mechanism, and modulation scheme appropriate to the distribution media. The common transport is seen as a "container" and facilitates the interoperability of the signal through different delivery media. This results in a common data stream after demodulation in the receiver, which simplifies the complexity of the receiver appliance. Studies conducted by ITU-R Working Party 10-11S support this container approach and further suggest that the same framing, synchronization, randomization, and inner and outer coding and interleaving mechanisms could be applied to all media.[12]

SATELLITE BROADCASTING

The Evolution Toward Digital Systems

The 1977 World Administrative Radio Conference (WARC-77) established an ITU frequency plan which regulates the use of broadcasting satellite services (BSS) in the frequency bands 11.7–12.5 GHz (for Region 1) and 11.7–12.2 GHz (for Region 3). In general, the plan assigned five channels to each country, based on frequency modulation (FM) of the analog conventional television systems used and provided for one FM sound subcarrier.[13] Since 1977, advanced analog television systems such as the European MAC/packet family and the Japanese MUSE system have been developed for the purpose of providing wide-screen format (16:9 aspect ratio), high-definition services with digital sound. These systems used analog compression techniques to operate in accordance with the Appendix 30 provisions.

The rationale for the evolution from an analog-based infrastructure to a digital satellite television system is compelling. The growing interest and advantages in digital picture and sound coding and the ability to provide multiprogramming services per transponder led ITU-R Working Party 10-11S to draft a new Recommendation to provide multiprogram picture, sound, and data services in the 11/12-GHz frequency range.[14] The adoption of digital modulation techniques with their superior interference protection characteristics allows reduction of the power requirements on the satellite and/or reduction of the size and gain of the receiver antenna. The use of digital picture and sound coding and compression technology allows an increase in the number of programs offered per satellite transponder, assuming narrowband channel assignments. For instance, each WARC-77 channel assigned to a service area could support a 60-Mbits/s useful bit rate assuming a TCM-8 PSK (2/3) modulation scheme. The TCM-8 PSK modulation scheme complies with the co-channel and adjacent-channel interference protection ratios established by the WARC-77 plan for analog systems. A 60-Mbits/s data rate is capable of supporting either one or two HDTV program services (each with a multichannel sound service) at between 30 and 45 Mbits/s per program,[15] up to five enhanced-definition television (EDTV) wide-screen services at 11 Mbits/s each, 11 SDTV program services at 5.5 Mbits/s each,[16] or 15 VHS-quality program services at 4.0 Mbits/s each. Table 11-1 provides examples of the protection ratios for analog and digital systems, assuming a C/N of 30 dB (threshold of visibility for analog systems) and a 60-Mbits/s data rate for digital systems, which is supportable at a C/N of 30 dB.

Table 11-1. Protection Ratios for Analog and Digital Systems in a WARC-77 Channel Matrix.

Wanted Signal	Unwanted Signal	Co-channel Ratio	Adjacent-Channel Ratio
PAL/FM	PSK	25 (19)	14 (11)
D2-MAC	PSK	23 (18)	15 (12)
8-PSK TCM 2/3	D2-MAC	17 (17)	11 (13.5)
8-PSK TCM 2/3	PSK	16	11.5

Notes:

1. For analog systems (PAL/FM and D2-MAC), a frequency deviation of 13.5 MHz/V is normally used. Figures in parentheses refer to a frequency deviation of 22 MHz/V and 33 MHz receiver bandwidth.

2. The modulator symbol rate for the digital systems (PSK and 8-PSK) is 30 Mbauds).

A digital narrowband system for use in the 11/12-GHz band based on MPEG-2[17] image and audio coding, transport multiplexing, and a service information system is under consideration as a European Technical Standard (ETS).[18]

Broadcasting-Satellite Service for Wide-RF-Band High-Definition Television

The function of the wide-band HDTV interface is to provide "transparent" HDTV transmission, that is, conserving the HDTV picture quality gathered at the source and reproducing those pictures on a large screen so that the reception quality is the same as found in the studio by providing a virtually transparent transmission path to the receiver. Progress in HDTV signal processing made by the end of 1992 enabled such a reduction in the bit rate so that no more than approximately 110 Mbits/s were required to transmit from a "transparent" channel. This had been demonstrated by numerous rigorous experiments. For the simultaneous transmission of video signals with sound, code protection, and other signals, a standard 140-Mbits/s digital channel could be used.[19] The progress in this area was reflected in Recommendation 788 prepared by Joint Working Party (JWP) 10-11/S, chaired by Mr. R. Zeitoun (Canada), vice chairman of Study Group 11.

Various applications were reported for the use of this broadcasting-satellite service for wide-RF-band high-definition television. The applications included television cinemas/video theaters with large HDTV screens.

Typical Digital Satellite System[20]

A model of a digital satellite system is shown in the Figure 11-1 functional block diagram. In this example, the system translates the output of the MPEG-2 transport stream multiplexer to a signal appropriate for a satellite channel. Although the following system description, based on European Telecommunication Standards,[21] assumes a single carrier per transponder with multiple services carried as packetized data in the time-division multiplex (TDM) of the transport data stream, multicarrier systems using frequency-division multiplex (FDM) techniques, each carrying a transport data stream, are also possible.

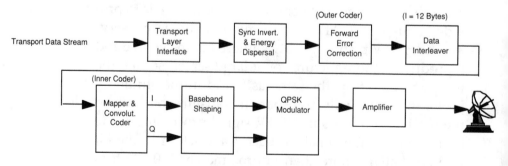

Figure 11-1. Satellite System Encoder Block Diagram.

In general, the input transport data stream can be organized as fixed-length packets as described for DTTB applications. In the MPEG-2 system, the transport multiplex packet consists of 188 bytes of data including a single sync-word byte (47H = 0100 0111). The first step is to randomize the data to ensure adequate binary transitions to comply with ITU Radio regulations. The data are randomized by a pseudo-random sequence polynomial generator (= $X^{15} + X^{14} + 1$) as shown in Figure 11-2, with the generator initialized to a value 00A9H [= (MSB)000 0000 1010 1001] every eight transport packets. All bytes of the transport stream are randomized with the exception of the sync bytes. The receiver descrambler is provided with an initialization signal by forcing an inversion of the sync byte in the first transport packet in the group of eight to a value of B8H (= inverse of 47H). This inverted sync byte is followed by the first (MSB) bit of the first byte from the pseudo-random-sequence generator. The randomization process continues even when the bit stream is absent or does not conform to the MPEG-2 transport stream format, to ensure that the carrier is properly modulated.

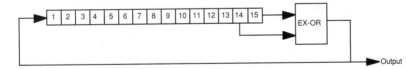

Figure 11-2. Random-Sequence Generator.

As with the DTTB system solution, a concatenation of convolutional (inner codes) and Reed–Solomon forward error correction (outer codes) is used to achieve ruggedness against noise and interference. The convolutional code can be configured to optimize system performance for a given satellite transponder bandwidth. In the European system, a Reed–Solomon RS(204,188, T = 8) shortened code from the RS(255,239, T = 8) code is applied to each randomized transport packet of 188 bytes (including the sync byte or inverted sync byte) and generates an error-protected packet as shown in Figure 11-3. Convolutional interleaving with depth I = 12 is applied to the error-protected packets to produce an interleaved frame. The interleaver can be composed of 12 branches, cyclically connected to the input byte stream. Each branch is assumed to be an FIFO (first-in, first-out) shift register of depth (M, j) cells (where M = N). Here N = 204, the length of the error-protected frame; I = 12, the interleaving depth; and j = branch index. The cells of the FIFO contain 1 byte and the input and output switchers are synchronized. In the sample implementation, the sync bytes (and inverted sync bytes) are always routed to branch "0" of the interleaver, which corresponds to a zero delay.

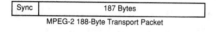

MPEG-2 188-Byte Transport Packet

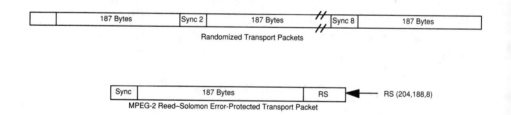

Figure 11-3. Protected Transport Packet.

The sample system employs a conventional Gray-coded QPSK modulator with absolute mapping as shown in Figure 11-4. Prior to modulation, the baseband I and Q signals are processed through a square-root raised cosine filter with a roll-off factor (a) of 0.35.

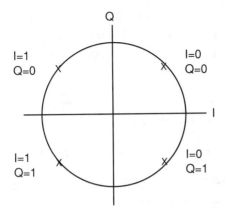

Figure 11-4. QPSK Constellation.

HARMONIZATION WITH ATM AND OTHER SWITCHED DATA SERVICES

The process of communicating information has been described in the globally accepted seven-layer open systems interconnection (OSI) model documented by the International Standards Organization (ISO). The seven layers are described in Table 11-2.

The mechanism for transporting data from one point to another in most communication systems includes identification of the source and destination. This information is critical in switched data services where data packets are moved from switching point node to node until the final destination is reached. In complex communication systems, data packets related to a single message may take different paths from the source to the destination, depending on the traffic load within the system. A packet intended for use at the data link and physical levels typically consists of six elements as shown in Figure 11-5. The six elements include start-of-packet **Flags** and synchronization information; **Frame-Control** information identifying the type of frame, such as data-carrying (payload) or control-information-carrying; identification of the transmission point, termed the

Source Address; identification of the receiving point, termed the **Destination Address**; the **Payload**; and an error-detection mechanism such as cyclical redundancy check (**CRC**) bits.

Flag(s) & Sync	Frame Control	Source Address	Destination Address	Payload	CRC

Figure 11-5. Generic Communications Packet.

Table 11-2. OSI Reference Model for Communication Protocols.

Layer	Layer Functions
Application	Provides service elements to process exchanged information services including: resource sharing, file transfer, database management
Presentation	Provides services necessary to format exchanged data and manage session dialog
Session	Establishes and terminates connections, arbitrates user rights to services; synchronizes data transfers
Transport	Provides functionality for error-free delivery of messages including: flow-control, error recovery, acknowledgment
Network	Provides transparent routing of messages between two transport entities
Datalink	Provides rules for transmission on the physical medium including: packet formats, access rights, and error detection and correction
Physical	Provides mechanical- and electrical-level interconnection

An industry standard for efficiently transporting video, sound, and data across switched networks at high data rates has been developed and is known as the *asynchronous transfer mode* (ATM) communications protocol. The ATM system was developed to accommodate mixing of different types of traffic within the same system. The ATM packet is based on a 53-byte cell consisting of two parts: a 5-byte header and a 48-byte information field, as shown in Figure 11-6. The header was designed for network functions and consists of six fields:

GFC: Generic flow-control 4-bit field used to control the flow of traffic across the user network interface

VPI: Virtual path finder 8-bit field

VCI: Virtual channel identifier 16-bit field. The VCI and VPI function together to provide the routing information to move the cells from one mode to the next. The information specific to the original source and final destination are not carried in the ATM header but are specified by the sequence of routing steps determined when the ATM channel is established.

PTI: Payload-type indicator 3-bit field

CLP: Cell loss priority 1-bit flag which establishes the cell's eligibility for discard by the network under congested conditions

HEC: Header-error control 8-bit field for ATM header-error correction

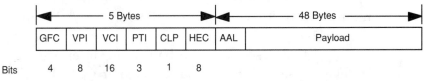

GFC = Generic Flow-Control Field AAL = 0-4 Byte Adaptation Layer
VPI = Virtual Path Finder Payload = User Information = 48-AAL Bytes
VCI = Virtual Channel Identifier
PTI = Payload-Type Indicator
CLP = Cell Loss Priority Indicator
HEC = Header-Error Control Field

Figure 11-6. ATM Cell.

The ATM 48-byte payload may be optionally segmented in such a way that up to 4 bytes can be allocated as AAL (ATM adaptation layer) bytes. The ATM packet, therefore, meets all of the needs associated with the generic data packet described in Figure 11-5.

Digital terrestrial television broadcasting is essentially a point-to-multipoint transmission system, and the MPEG-2 transport system has been designed as an efficient container for the video, sound, and data services that will be carried from the source to the consumer. Because the path between the source and consumers is essentially "fixed" (if the problems of multipath interference are set aside) and the data capacity of the terrestrial channel is severely constrained, there is no need to carry the source and destination or node information within each packet.

However, because the ATM protocol appears also to be an efficient mechanism for delivering video, sound, and associated ancillary data programming services over the types of switched networks envisioned for accommodating the requirements of the future global information infrastructure, a mechanism for facilitating translation from one packet structure to the other was deemed desirable by ITU-R Task Group 11/3. Such a system would also accommodate the broadcasters' requirements for contribution networks, as shown in Figure 11-7.

Figure 11-8 describes a mechanism for interfacing the MPEG-2 system 188-byte packet format with the ATM 53-byte format at the AAL-5 level. Two MPEG-2 transport packets contain 376 bytes of information. The 376 bytes can be transported within 8 ATM cells with 8-bytes of free data space left available for other use. This 8-byte trailer could be used to transport application-dependent information and actual payload-length information, and provide additional error protection such as a 32-bit CRC. The sum total is 384 bytes, which, as noted, is equal to the payload of 8 ATM cells at 48 bytes per cell.

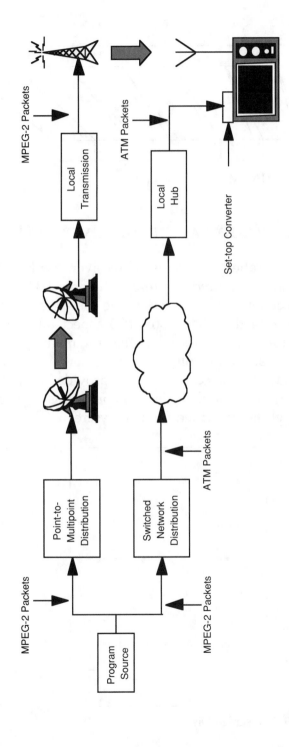

Figure 11-7. Television Contribution Networks.

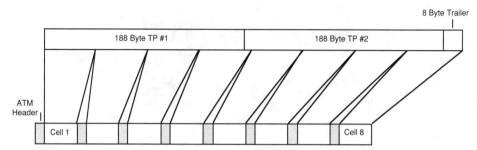

Figure 11-8. ATM–MPEG Translation.

HARMONIZATION AT THE RECEIVER LEVEL

A new generation of television receivers with a 16:9 aspect ratio is required to present the new HDTV and wide-screen television services to the consumer.

Recognizing that the existing 4:3 aspect ratio television services would be operational for many years to come, the first product offerings of the new wide-screen (16:9) aspect ratio receivers should provide compatible reception of conventional television programs. One technique suggested provided for a "polyscreen."[22]

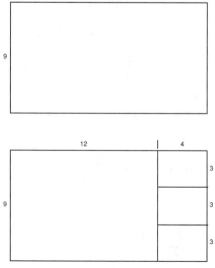

Figure 11-9. Polyscreen Display.

The polyscreen concept allowed a standard 4:3 aspect ratio picture to occupy a part of the screen of the wide-screen display, and three smaller-size 4:3 aspect ratio pictures then occupied the remainder, as shown in Figure 11-9. The additional display areas could be used for viewing additional channels, if sufficient tuner capacity was provided, or teletext or other captioning services. The concept of such windows is not foreign to the computer industry. Such a television receiver represents an important step in the introduction of these innovative systems and enables an evolutionary transition to new services.

The "polyscreen" approach makes it possible to view up to four programs simultaneously. The 16:9 format makes possible the presentation in its original form of wide-format cinematography.

Consumer expectations of what constitutes acceptable quality in a television service will become greater. Just as with the introduction of the CD into the sound services, consumers learned that additional dynamic range and a noise-free environment can be the norm. In view of such expectations, the new receivers would be expected to provide ghost image canceling, noise suppression, and a transparent scanning structure at a viewing distance of three times the picture height.

Harmonization at the receiver level goes beyond consideration of the display characteristics. The high level of interoperability provided by the use of digital technology can lead to an all-purpose consumer multimedia appliance. A generic block diagram of such a device is shown in Figure 11-10, and provides for both receipt of broadcasted services (via terrestrial, cable, or satellite means) and interfaces to traditional switched networks.

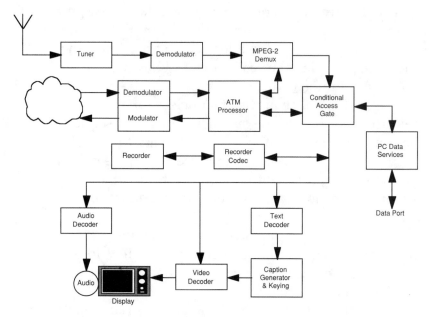

Figure 11-10. The DTTB Receiver Appliance.

Planning Factors and the Generic Receiver

The development of a DTTB service requires consideration of the planning factors, which includes the capabilities of the receiver to capture the modulated signal and accurately extract the data stream. The requirements placed on the digital receiver represent an advance in the application of technology (as compared to traditional analog receivers). The multi-carrier receiver developed for the COFDM-6 project[23] is an example of the application of the technology and is used here to describe how the receiver might process the DTTB signal.

The Tuner/Demodulator/Decoder may be divided into five subsections: the RF section, the demodulator analog IF/baseband section, the pre-FFT processor, the FFT block, and post-FFT signal reconstruction.

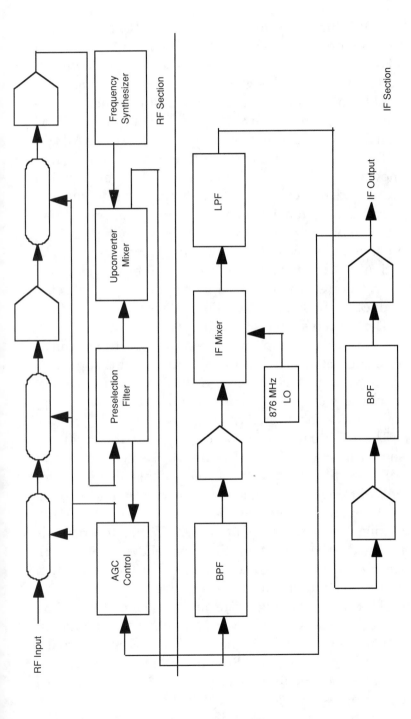

Figure 11-11. Tuner Block Diagram.

The RF tuner section of the Tuner/Demodulator/ Decoder provides channel selection within the UHF and VHF frequency bands. The tuner receives and downconverts the received signal via a high-side injection, double-conversion process with a first intermediate frequency (IF) centered at 920 MHz. The original COFDM signal is then translated to an IF centered at 44.0 MHz.

The RF input is applied to a three-stage attenuator, as shown in Figure 11-11. Three stages of RF **attenuation** are provided at the RF front end to fulfill system dynamic range requirements. These three stages provide an attenuation range of 6–45 dB. As shown in Figure 11-11, an attenuation stage is followed by a low-noise amplification (**LNA**) which in turn is followed by two stages of attenuation and an RF amplifier prior to the signal being applied to the **Preselection Filter** stage.

The filtered signal is tapped by a 3-dB power divider. One output of the tap is used to control the tuner gain as a function of level, while the second output is applied to the first-stage **Up-converter Mixer**. With this control loop, the gain will be determined mainly by strong signals outside the desired channel.

The RF section is followed by a first IF section, as shown in Figure 11-11. The first IF section includes a bandpass filter (**BPF**). The purpose of this filter is to suppress strong out-of-band signals, the IF image band (829–835 MHz), and LO leakage at 977–1723 MHz. During the conversion up to 920 MHz, the band is reversed. The bandpass filter is followed by an **IF Amplifier** stage which compensates for the attenuation in the filter and the mixer. The **IF Mixer** converts the 920-MHz IF signal band down to an IF centered at 44.0 MHz using a fixed LO at 876 MHz amplified to a minimum signal level of +17 dBm. The signal then is applied to the final low-pass filter (**LPF**) and IF amplifier stages (**IF AMP**), which are designed to amplify the desired signal and suppress spurious signals in the adjacent channels. At the IF output the signal is tapped a second time. The second tapped signal is used to control the tuner gain as a function of the desired signal and not be strong spurious signals.

The two-step conversion process, therefore, takes the RF signal (VHF and UHF bands) and converts it up to a fixed IF frequency at 920 MHz, which in turn is converted down to 44 MHz.

Pre-FFT Processor

The input signal to the decoder is the IF signal centered at 44 MHz. The task of the **AGC Amplifier** is to provide a signal with an amplitude such that a correct level is applied to the **A/D Converters**. The signal is down-converted to baseband using a quadrature LO signal at 44 MHz. The resulting complex analog baseband signal is then applied to the A/D converters, as shown in Figure 11-12.

With the normal behavior of the amplification/attenuation stages and the automatic gain control, the IF output signal will be controlled to –16 dBm for an RF input between –52 dBm and –5 dBm. A "weak signal" (–68 dBm) would then produce an IF output of –32 dBm. This "weak signal" is still properly handled by the pre-FFT processor AGC stage, which provides valid operation for IF input signals as low as –40 dBm.

The sample clock to the A/D converters is generated using a digital numerically controlled oscillator (**NCO**). The digital output signal from the NCO is D/A converted, low-pass filtered, and converted back to a digital signal by means of a hard limiter. The frequency of the sampling clock is controlled using a software phase-locked loop in the signal processor that is in the pre-FFT processor.

The output bit clock is also generated using the same type of NCO. The output bit-clock frequency is connected to the sampling clock frequency via a rational number which is dependent on the parameter setting in the modem.

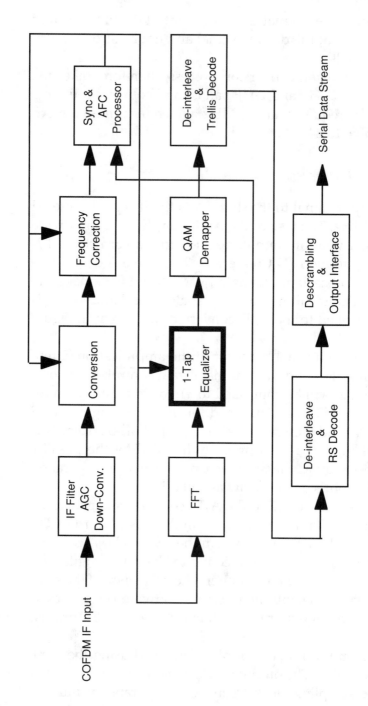

Figure 11-12. Demodulator/Decoder Block Diagram.

A **Frame Structure Generator** supplies *Tags* which define the start of the COFDM symbols and frames, and guard time suppression. The frame structure generator includes decimation and correlation circuits that assist the generator in its decision-making process. The next stage is the shifter and sync and AFC processor (**S-PROC**), which shifts the resulting signal spectrum up $f_s/2$ to avoid "negative frequencies" for the FFT processor, removes the guard interval, and provides control signals to the prior stages. The outputs of the S-PROC are complex frequency-shifted vectors and the frame tags.

FFT Block

The task of the FFT block is to perform a complex FFT on the input data. In the COFDM-6 receiver, the transform is calculated using two sets of processors in cascade. The first stage makes a 16-point transform. The second transform is programmable between 16 and 1024. The one-dimensional input data is gathered into a table and reorganized as an L x M array. The transform is first performed along the columns of the input array. Data from the first transform is adjusted by the factor $\exp(-j2\pi ms/N)$ and the second transform is taken along the rows of the array from the first transform.

Post-FFT Signal Reconstruction

After the FFT block, channel and phase correction takes place. Active carriers are latched into a register, null carriers are disregarded. Selection is based on the active carrier tag supplied with the data stream. The active carriers are passed on to chirp phase estimate and channel estimate arithmetic units and are subjected to phase and channel correction/equalization.

The resulting complex vectors are subjected to **QAM-Vector Demapping** (demodulated), followed by frequency de-interleaving and error correction. The QAM demapper consists mainly of a look-up table in memory. The digital "real" and "imaginary" values coming from the equalizer are used to address the memory. The contents of the memory are such that the memory outputs the relevant soft decision data to the **Trellis De-interleaving and Decoding** block.

Appropriate de-interleaving takes place followed by Trellis decoding. After the Trellis de-interleaver and decoder and prior to the Reed–Solomon de-interleaver and decoder, the symbols are repacked (**Symbol to Byte Packer**) into a byte-wide data stream to accommodate the functionality of the remaining circuitry. The **Reed-Solomon decoder** corrects any errors and reports any uncorrectable messages. The **Descrambler** reverses the function of the transmitter scrambler and provides the restored serial, transport-packetized data stream. The final **Interface** stage supplies an output serial bit stream at appropriate levels.

The generic receiver, therefore, can supply many of the resources, such as the Reed–Solomon and Trellis decoder error correction mechanisms, and the video and audio decoders, necessary to accommodate demodulated data streams supplied via other sources such as over satellite feeds or by ATM sourced telephony feeds.

HARMONIZATION WITH RECORDING TECHNOLOGY

New ITU-R Recommendations relating to recording contributed considerably to the progress in the field of HDTV. They dealt with the recording of HDTV images on film and the international exchange of programs electronically produced by means of high-definition television. The study of HDTV recording technology was assigned to the Joint Working Party (JIWP) 10-11R, chaired by Dr. P. Zaccarian (Italy).

The digital HDTV VTR was seen as being both an essential part of the HDTV production chain and the most difficult recording media challenge given the data rates required. An uncompressed high-definition television digital recorder must have the capacity to record at a rate of approximately 1200 Mbits/s. Digital recorders with that capacity have important application in non-broadcast uses. Reduced-bit-rate formats, including systems at low bit rates (in the area of 20 Mbits/s), implied by a fully compressed picture are required to complete the requirements of both industry and the consumer.

A 1200-Mbits/s recorder based on a 1-in. reel-to-reel transport using metal-particle tape and exhibiting a full range of features including shuttle and editing features has been demonstrated. The transport mechanism used is an adaptation of the 1-in. C-format. The sampling frequencies were 74.25 MHz for the luminance channel and 37.125 MHz for the two color-difference channels. Up to eight digital audio channels can be accommodated. The electronic interface standard for this tape transport is defined by SMPTE standards 240M and 260M. A 19-mm-cassette HDTV tape format standard (D6) was established in 1994 by SMPTE; it is also compatible with the electronic interface defined by the SMPTE 240M and 260M standards.[24]

Consumer-use recorders have also been demonstrated for recording and playback of both the MUSE and HD-MAC signals. A MUSE VCR for consumer use was developed based on a 1/2-in. transport and metal-particle tape. The HD-MAC system implementation utilized an improved VHS transport employing 1/2-in. metal-particle tape and achieving a signal bandwidth of 10.125 MHz (–6 dB) by using four heads, two frequency-modulated recording channels, and digital video and audio processing.[25]

Professional recorders based on the D1, D2, and D3 digital-tape formats with wide-screen (16:9) aspect ratio recording capabilities appeared in the market in 1993 and 1994.

Clearly, the most practical solution to recording and playback of advanced television services would be recorders which interface directly to the MPEG-2 transport stream. By the end of 1994, prototype systems based on a 6-mm-tape format and designed for both the professional and consumer markets had been demonstrated.

END NOTES

1. CCIR Document 11/716, "Summary Record of the Third Meeting," 13 October 1989, p. 4.

2. CCIR Report 624-3 (Mod. F) "Characteristics of Television Systems."

3. M.I. Krivocheev, "Summary of international standards activities," NAB HDTV World Conference, Las Vegas, Nevada, 16 April 1991, pp. 5–7.

4. M.I. Krivocheev, International trends in HDTV, 27th Electronic Industry Technical Conference, Tokyo, 5 October 1990.

5. M.I. Krivocheev, "Mark Krivocheev Suggests a New System to Deal with Different International Bandwidths," *Television* (April 1991), p. 7.

6. M.I. Krivocheev, "Television and Nothing but Television," *Cinema and Television Technology*, No. 10, XI (1991).

7. CCIR Document 11/122, "Report of the Chairman," 31 March 1992, p. 3.

8. European Telecommunications Draft Standard, prETS 300 468, "Digital Broadcasting Systems for Television, Sound, and Data Services: Specification for Service Information (SI) in Digital Video Broadcasting (DVB) Systems," November 1994.

9. European Telecommunications Draft Standard, prETS 300 429, "Digital Broadcasting Systems for Television, Sound, and Data Services: Framing Structure, Channel Coding, and Modulation: Cable Systems," August 1994.

10. European Telecommunications Draft Standard, prETS 300 421, "Digital Broadcasting Systems for Television, Sound, and Data Services: Framing Structure, Channel Coding, and Modulation for 11/12 GHz Satellite Services," August 1994.

11. European Telecommunications Draft Report, ETR 154, "Digital Broadcasting Systems for Television: Implementation Guidelines for the Use of MPEG-2 Systems: Video and Audio in Satellite and Cable Broadcasting Applications," November 1994.

12. ITU-R Document 10-11S/TEMP/26, "Digital Multi-programme Television Broadcast by Satellite," 28 November 1994.

13. Appendix 30 of the Radio Regulations provides for use of modulation systems with other characteristics provided that the use of such characteristics does not cause greater interference than that caused by the system considered in the appropriate Regional Plan.

14. Document 10-11S/TEMP/14, Draft New Recommendation, "Digital Multi-Programme Emission Systems for Television, Sound and Data Services for Satellites Operating in the 11/12 GHz Frequency Range," 25 November 1994.

15. Assuming QPSK modulation and rate 3/4 FEC.

16. ITU-R Document 10-11S/TEMP/26(Rev. 2), "Reply to Liaison Statements from Working Party B," 28 November 1994.

17. ISO/IEC International Standard 13818.

18. Document prETS 300 421, European Telecommunication Standards, "Digital Broadcasting Systems for Television, Sound and Data Services: Framing Structure, Channel Coding and Modulation for 11/12 GHz Satellite Services," July 1994.

19. CCIR Recommendation 788, "Coding Rate for Virtually Transparent Studio Quality Wide-RF Band HDTV Emissions in the Broadcasting-Satellite Service.

20. As described in document ITU-R 10-11S/14, October 1994.

21. Document prETS 300 421, European Telecommunication Standard, "Digital Broadcasting Systems for Television, Sound and Data Services: Framing Structure, Channel Coding and Modulation for 11/12 GHz Satellite Services," August 1994.

22. M.I. Krivocheev, "The First Twenty Years of HDTV: 1972–1992," SMPTE, 1993.

23. COFDM-6 System Technical Description, 11 July 1995.

24. SMPTE 277, For Television Digital Recording, 19 mm, Type D-6, Helical Data, Longitudinal Index, Cue, and Control Records, 1995.

25. W. Weissensteiner, "Concept of a Consumer-type HD-MAC VCR," IEE Conference Publication No. 293, International Broadcasting Convention, Brighton, U.K., 1988, pp. 228–230.

12

Conclusion: Communications in the 21st Century

THE COMMUNICATIONS INFRASTRUCTURE

When the world community last addressed the issue of television broadcasting standards, in the 1950s and 1960s, the work was conducted in a fairly constrained environment. Television was perceived as a service that stood alone. At that time, the challenge was to transport moving images and associated sound services from a central point to a community of consumers. The consumer appliance was a receiver. It came in various sizes of displays with one or more channels of sound. The dominant "interactive" communications media was the telephone, offering only two-way voice communications.

But television technology has not remained static. More than 40 years ago, the NTSC-compatible color system was demonstrated in the existing 6-MHz channels. The 25th anniversary of the introduction of color television services in Europe was celebrated in 1992. In 1992, digital high-definition television (HDTV) was being demonstrated in the same channels and work to establish a standard was under way. On 25 November 1991, 20 years after Japan initiated HDTV work in the CCIR, NHK (Japan) began regular program service using the 1125-line HDTV system. In February 1992, the 1250-line HDTV standard was used to broadcast the Albertville Olympic Games. These advancements were seen to have a substantial economic impact, considering that over 1000 million television sets are in the hands of consumers worldwide.

The level of program quality that can be achieved with the existing color television systems meets the basic needs for television broadcasting information and entertainment services. Before any new service can achieve widespread acceptance, it must provide a substantially greater viewing experience, offering a wide range of technical and service improvements. The new service must provide not only improved image and sound quality but also provide the consumer with attractive services that will stimulate the acquisition of new receivers and other consumer appliances. Only if both the technical and content improvements are compelling will consumers make the necessary economic commitments sufficient to cover the cost of developing and implementing the new service infrastructure. To achieve the necessary critical economic mass to drive this new environment, the broadcast, satellite, and cable distribution technologies and the program content must be appropriate for a global audience.[1] It is in the best interests of the consumer and the service provider alike that the technology employed be based on a common family of encoding and a common transport mechanism. A common mechanism provides the necessary volume to produce low-cost service solutions and forms the basis of a global information infrastructure.

The communications environment of the 21st century promises to allow a broader diversity of services and opportunities for the public based on a global information infrastructure. In September 1993, the United States Administration issued "The National Information Infrastructure: Agenda for Action," which unveiled a National Information Infrastructure (NII) initiative. Responses to this initiative by other Administrations throughout the world in the form of regional initiatives quickly followed, and the concept of global information infrastructures became the point of focus. A digitally based global communications system is seen as a mechanism that will unleash an information revolution. Television and telephone services will no longer each exist in an insular environment. They will become a part of a complex infrastructure that bridges technologies, industries, transport media, and applications. The consumer's appliance may just as likely be a personal computer as a television receiver. The all-digital communications system coupled with evolutionary advances in display technology for the consumer environment could provide all the tools necessary to create a fully integrated information society by the beginning of the 21st century.

The International Telecommunications Union recognizes the emergence of this new environment and has risen to the occasion. From the ITU's perspective, a strong and healthy multimedia global information infrastructure already exists. Broadcast television is seen as the major component of today's multimedia information flow to the world's consumers. In an increasingly mobile society, the information infrastructure must consist of both wired and wireless components. The work of the ITU shows that the technology necessary to support the wireless component, based on digital terrestrial television broadcasting (DTTB) technology, is available today.

The development of the DTTB system has focused on technology that allows for a wide variety of services in an integrated and interoperable environment and embraces the following principles:

- **Diversity of services**: There should be no constraint on the types of imaging, sound, and data services that can be provided (limited only by the total bit rate or data capacity of the system).
- **Interoperability**: There should be no constraint on service flexibility. The system should enable useful and cost-effective interchange of electronic image, sound, and data among different applications, among different industries, and among different performance levels.
- **Extensibility**: There should be no constraint on the ability to grow into new services, thus providing protection against obsolescence.

The adoption of these principles, particularly extensibility, lessens the significance of the level of maturity of the technology, opening up an opportunity for early adoption of standards prior to serious local investments in infrastructure.

The technology required for the complex signal processing involved in the broadcast chain, from the production requirements through distribution and emission, continues to develop at a feverish pace. In this environment, it becomes increasingly important to maintain a global view of the production, distribution, and emission chain as a whole while pursuing technological developments relating to particular areas of the signal chain. By doing so, the work of the ITU-R ensures compatibility of all of the elements of the communication's chain, that is, source coding, channel coding, modulation methods, terrestrial and satellite transmitters, cable television networks, receivers, and so forth.

One of the main features offered by digital technology is a more efficient use of the spectrum, whether that spectrum is contained within a wireless channel, the bandwidth of a recording medium, or the bandwidth of a copper wire or an optical fiber. More efficient use of the spectrum leads to room for more services. More efficient use of the spectrum leads to more diversity in the services offered. Digital packetized communications systems employing headers and compression technology can provide flexibility, economy, and compatibility across a broad range of distribution media, thereby allowing development of new services and the practical possibility of a myriad of entertainment, education, information, and transactional services.

The ITU-R has responded to the emerging advances in the application of technology. On emission topics, the ITU-R has directed efforts in terrestrial and satellite broadcasting, data broadcasting, and baseband formats. In the area of program exchange, consideration was given to baseband signal formats, video tape and video disk, and film and telecine standards and to digital data streams that allow the information to be transported across different media.

The world technical community understands that terrestrial broadcasting, as the most ubiquitous and cost-effective means of providing services to the consumer, is the key to the introduction of digital services. In North America, Europe, and countries of the Pacific Rim, local regulatory agencies are considering mechanisms that allow terrestrial broadcasters the flexibility of offering multichannel services within their existing VHF/UHF channel assignments as a means of coping with competitive cable and satellite services to ensure the viability of the terrestrial broadcasting services and to promote diversity of services.[2] The International Telecommunications Union is addressing the harmonization of digital methods for delivery of services to the home.[3] The ITU, in searching for a coordinated approach to the development of such delivery systems, has focused on source coding and transport mechanisms based on common processing algorithms and having a maximum of shared parameters.

In his report[4] of the work of Study Group 11 for the period March 1994 to May 1995, the chairman of Study Group 11 commented that a new era in television broadcasting was emerging, marked by the emergence of fully digital production and delivery systems and based on the extensive development work required to make HDTV an economically feasible and deployable service. He predicted that the broadcasting environment of the future would include not only conventional television, but also enhanced and high-definition television, in both analog and digital forms, delivered over terrestrial and satellite transmitters, and further that some digital transmissions would also contain multiple program streams including data. Data services would include both program-related and independent data services, giving new meaning to broadcast delivery.

New television systems will be developed, new frequency agile displays will be designed, and new services will be created to take advantage of the challenges of this new environment and to bring viewers globally the benefits of the new era. In the planning and implementation of these new systems and services, it is necessary to consider not only the new opportunities presented by these technical developments but also the constraints imposed by the current investment in the infrastructure. There are, today, over 1000 million television receivers in use and thousands of broadcasting facilities in operation providing services for those receivers throughout the world. It is thus necessary to be relatively conservative in planning the new systems and services so that the existing end-users, the consumers, are not disenfranchised. Digital standards introduce new challenges in planning and spectrum management. Consideration must be given to appropriate power levels, interference and sharing criteria, protection ratios for both the new digital services and the existing analog ones, and the necessary coordination among service providers, countries, and regions of the world. The chairman concluded:

There should be no doubt, however, that the results of this work to introduce digital systems for broadcasting will bring great benefits to broadcasters and viewers in the years ahead and that in the ongoing work of Study Group 11 lies a major responsibility to achieve the necessary balance among the conflicting requirements.

Today, we can acknowledge that television is one of the most widely available means of communication. Television is a tool for communication that not only serves as an entertainment medium but portrays the realities of life around our globe. Television has become a means of educating the masses, molding public opinion, and bringing humanity closer together. Those individuals working in the technology of television are constantly refining its capacity to meet service needs, to better its performance, and to provide new and powerful tools for new applications. At some point, the accumulation of improvements can be viewed as the next major step in an evolutionary process and result in the recognition of a new standard. The integrated communications infrastructure of the 21st century, based on digital technology, will be that new standard. The technology necessary to support that standard is available now.

THE INFORMATION AGE

In the 21st century, no nation or region of the world will be able to afford to allow communication services provided to its citizens to be second class as compared to services provided in the remainder of the world. In the coming age of information, advantages will accrue to "information-haves" societies to the detriment of the "information-have-not" societies.

The vision of this new age sees the citizen of the 21st century communicating with the world using an inexpensive personal communication appliance (PCA). The

PCA will support individual mobility by allowing this citizen of the world community to be contacted regardless of location. The same "personal contact number" will be able to be "dialed" anywhere in the world and contact the intended person independent of whether the person is at home, at work, or in transit. The PCA could allow the citizen of the world to retrieve data from the world's libraries, images from the world's museums, and sounds from the world's environment. Analog communications systems have allowed us to capture and share the world in which we live. The application of digital technology allows us also to synthesize, create, and share images and experiences that reside only in our imaginations. The PCA could also allow world citizens to act as sources, sharing their experiences and dreams with others.

The human character is tremendously diverse, having developed a broad spectrum of cultural traits and experiences. A world community that is able to communicate with and better understand its diverse constituencies is a world that is best equipped to both protect and maintain the individual cultural heritages. A world in which individuals can share their own cultures with others and develop an understanding of those other cultures is a world in which individuals can better develop respect for the worth of those other cultures. Armed with modern tools of communication, the world community will be better equipped to solve the global problems of the 21st century.

The ITU-R has met its commitment to provide the tools necessary to implement a global information infrastructure necessary to support the information age. The important results achieved by the ITU confirm its vitality as an international forum for communications activities. The ITU continues to play a dominant role in the new era of digital communications that will characterize the 21st century. The technologists have provided a set of tools that allow the world community to establish an inexpensive, integrated, ubiquitous, and extensible communications system. The question now is what we will choose to create with those tools.

END NOTES

1. M.I. Krivocheev, Progress and new studies in television broadcasting of interest to developing countries, World Telecommunication Conference, Buenos Aires, March 1994.

2. European Broadcasting Union, Document BSS 057, "Options for Digital Terrestrial Television," 14 April 1994.

3. ITU-R [Doc. 11/141], Draft New Recommendation, Document 11/BL/55-E, "Harmonization of Digital Methods for Delivery Systems for Television Services to the Home," 30 March 1994.

4. ITU Document 11/79, "Report of the Chairman of Study Group 11," 17 May 1995, p. 3.

Glossary of Terms

The following Glossary of Terms is offered as a quick reference and an aid to understanding the contents of the book. It should not be considered as complete.

access unit: A coded representation of a presentation unit. In the case of audio, an access unit is the coded representation of an audio frame. In the case of video, an access unit includes all the coded data for a picture, and any bit or byte stuffing that follows it, up to but not including the start of the next access unit. If a picture is not preceded by a `group_start_code` or a `sequence_header_code`, the access unit begins with the picture start code. If a picture is preceded by a `group_start_code` and/or a `sequence_header_code`, the access unit begins with the first byte of the first of these start codes. If it is the last picture preceding a `sequence_end_code` in the bit stream, all bytes between the last byte of the coded picture and the `sequence_end_code` (including the `sequence_end_code`) belong to the access unit.

ATV: Advanced Television System.

Bidirectional Pictures (B-pictures): Pictures that use both future and past pictures as a reference. This technique is termed *bidirectional prediction*. B-pictures provide the most compression. B-pictures do not propagate coding errors, as they are never used as a reference.

bit rate: The rate at which the compressed bit stream is delivered from the channel to the input of a decoder.

blocks: A block is an 8-by-8 array of pel values or DCT coefficients representing luminance or chrominance information.

bps: Bits per second.

byte-aligned: A bit in a coded bit stream is byte-aligned if its position is a multiple of 8 bits from the first bit in the stream.

CDTV: (*See* **Conventional Television Systems**.)

channel: A digital medium that stores or transports a digital bitstream.

chrominance: The color information, such as hue and saturation, in an imaging system. A sample, matrix, or block of samples representing the color-difference (Cr and Cb) representation of the image(s) and related to the primary colors in a manner defined in the bitstream.

coded representation: A data element as represented in its encoded form.

compression: Reduction in the number of bits used to represent an item of data.

constant bit rate: Operation in which the bit rate is constant from start to finish of the compressed bit stream.

Conventional Television System: Formerly used to signify the analog NTSC, PAL, and SECAM television systems as defined in ITU Recommendation 470; replaced by the term **Standard Television System**.

CRC: The Cyclic Redundancy Check to verify the correctness of the data.

data element: An item of data as represented before encoding and after decoding.

DC coefficient: The discrete cosine coefficient for which the frequency is zero in both directions.

DCT: Discrete Cosine Transform, an invertible orthogonal mathematical transform.

decoded stream: The decoded reconstruction of a compressed bit stream.

decoder: An embodiment of a decoding process.

decoding (process): The process that reads an input coded bit stream and outputs decoded pictures or audio samples.

decoding time stamp (DTS): A field that may be present in a PES packet header that indicates the time that an access unit is decoded in the system target decoder.

digital storage media (DSM): A digital storage or transmission device or system.

DSM-CC: Digital storage media command and control.

DTTB: Digital Terrestrial Television Broadcasting.

editing: A process by which one or more compressed bit streams are manipulated to produce a new compressed bit stream. Conforming edited bit streams are understood to meet the requirements defined by the bitstream.

EDTV quality: Implies that the potential exists for the delivery of a picture which is subjectively indistinguishable from the 4:2:2 level of ITU Recommendation 601. This quality shall be maintained for a given portion of television program material.

elementary stream (ES): A generic term for one of the coded video, coded audio, or other coded bit streams. One elementary stream is carried in a sequence of PES packets with one and only one `stream_id`.

Elementary Stream Clock Reference (ESCR): A time stamp in the PES Stream from which decoders of PES streams may derive timing.

encoder: An embodiment of an encoding process.

encoding (process): A process that reads a stream of input pictures or audio samples and produces a valid coded bit stream as defined by the bitstream.

entitlement control message (ECM): Entitlement control messages are private conditional access information that specify control words and possibly other stream-specific, scrambling, and/or control parameters.

entitlement management message (EMM): Entitlement management messages are private conditional access information that specify the authorization level or the services of specific decoders. They may be addressed to single decoders or groups of decoders.

entropy coding: Variable-length lossless coding of the digital representation of a signal to reduce redundancy.

entry point: Refers to a point in a coded bit stream after which a decoder can become properly initialized and commence syntactically correct decoding. The first transmitted picture after an entry point is either an I-picture or a P-picture. If the first transmitted picture is not an I-picture, the decoder may produce one or more pictures during acquisition.

event: Defined as a collection of elementary streams with a common time base, an associated start time, and an associated end time.

field: For an interlaced video signal, a field is the assembly of alternate lines of a frame. Therefore, an interlaced frame is composed of two fields: a top field and a bottom field.

forbidden: This term, when used in clauses defining the coded bit stream, indicates that the value shall never be used. This is usually to avoid emulation of start codes.

frame: A frame contains the lines of spatial information of a video signal. For progressive video, these lines contain samples starting from one time instant and continuing through successive lines to the bottom of the frame. For interlaced video, a frame consists of two fields: a top field and a bottom field. One of these fields will commence one field later than the other.

GOP: A Group of Pictures consists of one or more pictures in sequence.

HDTV: High-definition-television, having a resolution of approximately twice that of conventional television in both the horizontal (H) and vertical (V) dimensions and a picture aspect ratio (H x V) of 16:9.

HDTV quality: Implies that the potential exists for the delivery of a picture which is subjectively identical with the interlaced HDTV studio standard. Quality shall remain consistent with this for a given portion of television program material.

Intracoded Pictures (I-pictures): Coded using information present only in the picture itself and not dependent on information from other pictures. I-pictures provide a mechanism for random access into the compressed video data. I-pictures employ transform coding of the pel blocks and provide only moderate compression.

layer: One of the levels of the video and system specification in the data hierarchy.

LDTV quality: Quality equivalent to that obtainable with the MPEG-1 system, which operates on a source with resolution approximately 1/4 that of the 4:2:2 level of ITU Recommendation 601. This quality is considered to resemble that of VHS.

luminance: A sample, matrix, or block of samples representing the monochrome (black/white) representation of the image(s) and related to the primary colors in a manner defined in the bitstream.

macroblock: In the ATV system, a macroblock consists of four blocks of luminance and one each of the Cr and Cb blocks.

Mbps: 1 million bits per second.

MPEG: Standards developed by the ISO/IEC JTC1/SC29 WG11/602, **M**oving **P**icture **E**xperts **G**roup. MPEG may also refer to the Group.

MPEG-2: ISO standards 13818-1 (Systems), 13818-2 (Video), 13818-3 (Audio), 13818-4 (Conformance).

pack: Consists of a pack header followed by zero or more packets. It is a layer in the system coding syntax.

packet: Consists of a header followed by a number of contiguous bytes from an elementary data stream. It is a layer in the system coding syntax.

packet data: Contiguous bytes of data from an elementary data stream present in the packet.

packet identifier (PID): A unique integer value used to associate elementary streams of a program in a single or multiprogram Transport Stream.

padding: A method to adjust the average length of an audio frame in time to the duration of the corresponding PCM samples, by continuously adding a slot to the audio frame.

payload: Refers to the bytes which follow the header byte in a packet. For example, the payload of a Transport Stream packet includes the PES_packet_header and its PES_packet_data_bytes or pointer_field and PSI sections, or private data. However, a PES_packet_payload consists only of PES_packet_data_bytes. The Transport Stream packet header and adaptation fields are not payload.

PES: Packetized Elementary Stream.

PES packet: The data structure used to carry elementary stream data. It consists of a packet header followed by PES packet payload.

PES packet header: The leading fields in a PES packet up to but not including the PES_packet_data_byte fields in which the stream is not a padding stream. In the case of a padding stream, the PES packet header is defined as the leading fields in a PES packet up to but not including the padding_byte fields.

PES Stream: Consists of PES packets, all of whose payloads consist of data from a single elementary stream, and all of which have the same stream_id.

picture: Source, coded, or reconstructed image data. A source or reconstructed picture consists of three rectangular matrices representing the luminance and two chrominance signals.

Predicted Pictures (P-pictures): Coded with respect to the nearest *previous* I- or P-picture. This technique is termed *forward prediction*. P-pictures provide more compression than I-pictures and serve as a reference for future P-pictures or B-pictures. P-pictures can propagate coding errors when P-pictures (or B-pictures) are predicted from prior P-pictures in which the prediction is flawed.

presentation time stamp (PTS): A field that may be present in a PES packet header that indicates the time that a presentation unit is presented in the system target decoder.

presentation unit (PU): A decoded Audio Access Unit or a decoded picture.

program: A collection of program elements. Program elements may be elementary streams. Program elements need not have any defined time base; those that do have a common time base are intended for synchronized presentation.

Program Clock Reference (PCR): A time stamp in the Transport Stream from which decoder timing is derived.

program element: A generic term for one of the elementary streams or other data streams that may be included in the program.

Program Specific Information (PSI): Consists of normative data which are necessary for the demultiplexing of Transport Streams and the successful regeneration of programs.

Program Stream: The result of combining one or more streams of PES packets sharing a common time base into a single bit stream.

progressive: The property of pictures wherein all samples of the image (picture of frame) represent the same instant in time.

quantized data: As used in this book, data in which the number of bits used to represent the samples of information is reduced by a scale factor, increasing the coarseness of the individual sample representation.

random access: The process of beginning to read and decode the coded bit stream at an arbitrary point.

reserved: When used in clauses defining the coded bit stream, indicates that the value may be used in the future for extensions. Unless otherwise specified all reserved bits shall be understood to be set to "1."

scrambling: The alteration of the characteristics of a video, audio, or coded data stream in order to prevent unauthorized reception of the information in a clear form. This alteration is a specified process under the control of a conditional access system.

SDTV: (*See* **Standard Television System.**)

SDTV quality: Quality approximately equivalent to that of the current NTSC, PAL or SECAM systems. This equivalent quality may be achieved from pictures sourced at the 4:2:2 level of ITU Recommendation 601 and subjected to processing as part of the bit-rate compression. The results should be such that when judged across a representative sample of program material, subjective equivalence with NTSC, PAL, and SECAM is achieved.

slice: A series of consecutive macroblocks.

source stream: A single, nonmultiplexed stream of samples before compression coding.

splicing: The concatenation performed on the system level or two different elementary streams. It is understood that the resulting stream must conform totally to the ATSC Digital Television Standard.

Standard Television System: The analog NTSC, PAL and SECAM television systems as defined in ITU Recommendation 470.

start codes: 32-bit codes embedded in the coded bit stream that are unique. They are used for several purposes, including identifying some of the layers in the coding syntax. Start codes consist of a 24-bit prefix (0x000001) and an 8-bit `stream_id`.

STD input buffer: A first-in, first-out buffer at the input of a system target decoder for storage of compressed data from elementary streams before decoding.

still picture: A coded still picture consists of a video sequence containing exactly one coded picture that is intracoded. This picture has an associated PTS and the presentation time of succeeding pictures, if any, is later than that of the still picture by at least two picture periods.

stuffing bits/bytes: Code words that may be inserted into the coded bitstream and may be discarded during the decoding process. They result in an increase in the bit rate of the stream.

syntax: A set of rules within a programming language for denoting valid statements in that language.

system header: A data structure that carries information summarizing the system characteristics of the ATSC Digital Television Standard multiplexed bit stream.

System Clock Reference (SCR): A time stamp in the Program Stream from which decoders timing is derived.

system target decoder (STD): A hypothetical reference model of a decoding process used to describe the semantics of the ATSC Digital Television Standard multiplexed bit stream.

time stamp: A term that indicates the time of a specific action such as the arrival of a byte or the presentation of a presentation unit.

Transport Stream: The result of combining one or more programs with one or more independent time bases into a single bit stream.

Transport Stream packet header: The leading fields in a Transport Stream packet up to and including the `conti-nuity_counter` field.

variable bit rate: Operation in which the bit rate varies with time during the decoding of a compressed bit stream.

variable length coding (VLC): A reversible procedure for coding that assigns shorter code words to frequent events and longer code words to less frequent events.

video sequence: Represented by a Sequence Header, one or more Groups of Pictures, and an end-of-sequence code in the data stream.

Index

A

A/D (analog-to-digital) converters, 249
AAL (ATM adaptation layer),
28, 242
AC-3 system, 119–126
Access identification, conditional, 60
AGC amplifier, 249
AM (amplitude modulation),
140
Analysis filter bank, 105
Ancillary data, 22
Appliances, teleputer consumer,
198
ATM (asynchronous transfer
mode)
communications protocol,
240
switched data services, 231
technology development, 28
transport mechanism, 23
Audio
compression types and language identification, 58
how AC-3 codes, 119–126

how MPEG codes, 116–119
perceptual coding of multipath, 109–110
Audio signals, coding, 101–128
generic system description,
104–109
how AC-3 codes audio,
119–126
how MPEG codes audio,
116–119
perceptual coding of multipath audio, 109–110
sound services, 110–116

B

BER (bit error rate) measurement, 146–147, 223
Bits
allocator, 105
defined, 19
streams, 40
BPF (band-pass filter), 248
Broadcasting, 2–6
defined, 3
interactive television,
195–208

W